Tumbling Blocks

NEW QUILTS FROM AN OLD FAVORITE

American Quilter's Society

P. O. Box 3290 • Paducah, KY 42002-3290
www.AQSquilt.com

Located in Paducah, Kentucky, the American Quilter's Society (AQS) is dedicated to promoting the accomplishments of today's quilters. Through its publications and events, AQS strives to honor today's quiltmakers and their work and to inspire future creativity and innovation in quiltmaking.

EDITOR: BARBARA SMITH
GRAPHIC DESIGN: LYNDA SMITH
COVER DESIGN: MICHAEL BUCKINGHAM
PHOTOGRAPHY: CHARLES R. LYNCH

Library of Congress Cataloging-in-Publication Data

Tumbling blocks / edited by Barbara Smith.
    p. cm. -- (New quilts from an old favorite)
  ISBN 1-57432-789-5
  1. Patchwork--Patterns. 2. Quilting--Patterns. 3.   Patchwork
  quilts--Competitions--United States.   I. Smith, Barbara, 1941- II. Series.
    TT835 .T82 2002
      746.46'041--dc21
                                2002001508

Additional copies of this book may be ordered from the American Quilter's Society, PO Box 3290, Paducah, KY 42002-3290, or online at www.AQSquilt.com.

Dedication

This book is dedicated to all those
who view a traditional quilt and
see within it a link to the past
and a vision for the future.

Contents

Patterns

More Tumbling Blocks Patterns

The Museum

Preface

The role of a museum is more than preserving the past. Its highest service is performed as it links the past to the present and to the future. With that goal at heart, the Museum of the American Quilter's Society (MAQS) annually sponsors a contest and exhibit called *New Quilts from an Old Favorite*. Created to acknowledge our quiltmaking heritage and to recognize innovation, creativity, and excellence, the contest challenges today's quiltmakers to interpret a single traditional quilt block in a work of their own design. Each year, contestants respond with stunning interpretations, and this year is no exception. In these pages, you will find a brief description of the contest, followed by a presentation of the five award winners and the 13 finalists.

Full-color photographs of the quilts are accompanied by each quiltmaker's comments, providing insight into widely divergent creative processes. Full-sized templates for the traditional Tumbling Block are included in several sizes to form the basis for your interpretation. Tips, techniques, and patterns contributed by the contest winners and finalists offer an artistic framework for your own quilts.

Our wish is that *Tumbling Blocks: New Quilts from an Old Favorite* will further our quiltmaking heritage as new quilts based on the Tumbling Blocks pattern are inspired by the outstanding quilts, patterns, and instructions provided in this book.

The Contest

Annually, the MAQS contest, *New Quilts from an Old Favorite,* challenges quiltmakers to create innovative quilts from a single traditional block pattern. The choice for millennium year 2002 was Tumbling Blocks.

Although the contest encouraged "outside the box" creativity, there were some basic requirements for entries.

- Quilts were to be recognizable in some way as being related to the Tumbling Blocks pattern.
- Finished size of the quilt was a minimum of 50" in width and height but no more than 100".
- Quilting was required on each quilt entered in the contest.
- A quilt could be entered only by the person or group who made it.
- Each entry was to have been completed after December 31, 1996.
- Each contestant was asked to submit an entry form and two slides, one of the full quilt and another of a detail from it.

Three jurors viewed dozens of slides, deliberating over design, use of materials, interpretation of the theme, and technical excellence. Eventually, they narrowed the field of entries to 18 finalists, who were then invited to submit their quilts for judging.

With quilts by the 18 finalists in front of them, three judges meticulously examined the pieces, evaluating them again for design, innovation, theme, and workmanship. First through fifth place award winners were selected and notified.

Each year the contest winners and the finalists are featured in an exhibit that opens at the Museum of the American Quilter's Society in Paducah, Kentucky. Over a two-year period, the exhibit travels to a number of museums across North America and is viewed by thousands of quilt enthusiasts. Corporate sponsorship of the contest helps to underwrite the costs, enabling even smaller museums across the country to display the exhibit.

In addition, the contest winners and finalists are included in a beautiful book published annually by the American Quilter's Society. *Tumbling Blocks: New Quilts from an Old Favorite* is the ninth in the contest, exhibit, and publication series. It joins the previous traditional block design contests: *Double Wedding Ring*, *Log Cabin*, *Ohio Star*, *Kaleidoscope*, *Mariner's Compass*, *Pineapple*, *Storm at Sea*, and *Bear's Paw*.

For information about entering the next contest, write to Museum of the American Quilter's Society at PO Box 1540, Paducah, KY, 42002-1540; call (270) 442-8856; or visit MAQS online at www.quiltmuseum.org.

The traditional Tumbling Block is a hexagon divided into three equal diamonds. But, when the three diamonds are cut from fabrics with different values, a light, a medium, and a dark, something magical happens. They form a three-dimensional box. When the boxes are piled on top of each other, a mysterious structure forms that changes as you look at it, sometimes appearing like stacked boxes, sometimes like boxes hanging from the ceiling.

The finalists in this contest have pushed this simple hexagon shape even further to create wonderfully imaginative landscapes and graphic designs. The finalists artistically demonstrate that a shared tradition is only the beginning. They prove that, through variations in color, theme, and innovative design, the possibilities offered by the traditional Tumbling Blocks pattern are limited only by the imagination.

Winners

1st Place
Twist of Fate

Barbara Oliver Hartman
Flower Mound, Texas

2nd Place
Butterfly Houses

D. Nadine Ruggles
Pittsburgh, Pennsylvania

3rd Place
Tumbling Texas Two Step

Cindy Vough
Nicholasville, Kentucky

8

4th Place
Quilter's Block

Nancy Cluts
Sammamish, Washington

5th Place
Glass Magic Blocks

Shelly Stokes
Miltona, Minnesota

Tumbling Blocks: New Quilts from an Old Favorite

Finalists

The Day Our Stars Tumbled
Kathleen M. Andrews

Spin-Offs
Arleen Boyd

Blocks World
Lorrie Faith Cranor

United We Stand
Patricia C. Dowling

Everlasting Life
Yuki Fushiki

Block Party
Patricia Klem

Unwinding
Nancy Lambert

Stumbling Blocks
Barbara Schneider

Earth Shattering
Lucy Silliman

Tumbling Blocks
Janet Jo Smith

Let Freedom Ring
Judy Sogn

Cats and Mice
Carolyn F. Tesar

Stumbling Blocks
Cathryn Zeleny

9

Sponsors

Fairfield
Quality Polyester Products for Home and Industry

marcusbrothers
TEXTILES INCORPORATED

JANOME
Because You Simply Love To Sew ™

Tumbling Blocks: New Quilts from an Old Favorite

Twist of Fate

62" x 54"

By Barbara Oliver Hartman.

Tumbling Blocks: New Quilts from an Old Favorite

D OING THIS QUILT IS
SOMETHING I WOULD NOT
NORMALLY DO, SO IT MADE
ME THINK AND GET OUT
OF MY COMFORT ZONE.

Flower Mound, Texas

Barbara Oliver Hartman

Meet the quilter

I began quiltmaking about 20 years ago because I needed a hobby. Now, it has become the thing that I spend the most time doing. I work on quilts just about every day. A perfect day for me is going into my studio and spending the day. I take breaks for household duties, meals, etc. When my husband, Bob, comes home in the afternoon, we have dinner, then it's back to the studio where I stay until about 10 P.M. A perfect week is doing this seven days in a row. That unfortunately does not happen all the time. I am easily distracted and have the practical matters of life to deal with. I enjoy phone calls and lunches with my friends, who are all quilters. Mostly, I am a one-dimensional person who is totally possessed by what I do. Life is good!

Inspiration and design

To make this quilt, I used cotton fabrics that were hand-dyed or batiked. It is all pieced on a foundation. The batting is a wool and cotton blend.

It was fun to challenge myself by making this quilt for the contest, and the Tumbling Block has always been interesting to me. Doing this quilt is something I would not normally do, so it made me think and get out of my comfort zone.

While I was sewing the strips of the quilt together, my mother was undergoing treatment for lymphoma and was in the hospital from complications of the chemotherapy. After visiting her each day, I would go home and sew. The sewing was easy because all the design work and the thinking part were done. This was my therapy. I was accomplishing something and at the same time doing something very soothing.

For quilting this quilt, I decided on something simple. I machine quilted in the ditch and then quilted simple lines that radiated out from the central sphere. It was my idea that the sphere was the main focus of the quilt, and any secondary design would not benefit the quilt in any meaningful way and might be a distraction.

Creating distorted blocks

When first deciding to design and make this quilt, I started with my computer. Using one of my graphics programs, I drew a page of triangles and put them together in a tumbling-block fashion. I copied and pasted until the page was filled. Then using some of the special effects available, I started playing with ways to distort the blocks in an interesting manner. I really liked the spherical version and used a "twirl" feature to make a more complex and interesting design.

That was the easy part. Then came trying to figure the best way to construct it. Most of my piecing is done on a foundation, and that was the method that worked here. After shading in my drawing and coming up with a plan, I took the drawing to a photocopy store and enlarged the design to the desired size. To make it large enough, I had to cut it in half after about the third enlargement, enlarge both halves, and then tape it back together. Once I had the design at full size, I was able to begin the piecing.

Each row was numbered and drawn out on foundation fabric. It was pretty tricky because of the curves, but once I started, it got easier. Sometimes this got confusing because, when you put the strips up on the design wall to look at them, they are backward relative to the drawing. That takes some getting used to at first.

To make the design readable, I chose a palette of light, medium, and dark fabrics of certain colors, basically orange and purple with some greens and

golds in all hand-dyed and batik fabrics. I put them together in stacks according to value and then randomly picked from each group.

One decision I made, after making many of the strips, was to use one fabric for the background of the sphere instead of piecing the background as shown in the drawing on page 13. Not only would piecing the background be difficult, but the busy fabric would detract from the sphere, which was the intended focal point. I was lucky that I had a fabric for the background in my stash that happened to be a batik with the same pattern as one of the blocks. It worked perfectly.

Knowing the border must be very simple, I experimented with several possibilities. My first thought was to have none, and my second was to have just a dark binding. I knew it needed something, but a dark border around all four sides killed all the movement of the design. My solution was to put the border on two sides with little windows in the dark fabric to tie it all together.

Detail from TWIST OF FATE.

Detail from TWIST OF FATE.

Barbara's original computer drawing superimposed over the finished quilt.

Butterfly Houses

50" x 82"

By D. Nadine Ruggles.

Details from BUTTERFLY HOUSES.

Tumbling Blocks: New Quilts from an Old Favorite

D. Nadine Ruggles

Gerlingen, Germany

I LOVE THE CHALLENGE OF USING FABRICS TO ACHIEVE SPECIAL EFFECTS, LIKE DEPTH, LUMINOSITY, AND IRIDESCENCE IN MY QUILTS.

Meet the quilter

From a very young age, I have used fabric as a medium for expression. I began to make my own clothes when I was 12 years old. In high school, I made evening wear for proms and dances. Later, I worked for a fabric store that carried dressmaking fabrics and a small selection of quilting cottons and supplies. I was drawn to the quilting fabrics arranged by color on the shelves, and made my first quilt, a bargello wall hanging, in 1991. I began to experiment with patchwork clothing from Judy Murrah's *Jacket Jazz* series, combining my dressmaking skills and those gorgeous quilting cottons. Quilting became my focus in 1994 after moving to Germany. I wanted to make just one large quilt for the bed and, of course, couldn't stop quilting after that.

While living in Germany, I taught quilting classes for our local shop and served two terms as president of the Black Forest Quilters, a German-American quilting guild. I have learned so much by teaching others, and my students have inspired me to be more creative. I believe that there are no rules in quilting, only challenges.

I enjoy choosing fabrics, finding the perfect fabric for a certain block or pattern, and putting different colors and fabrics together to create new effects. Fabrics, patterns, other quilters, artists, authors, photos, nature, special occasions, room settings, and the Internet, among other things, have inspired me. I love to make all kinds of quilts, from country quilts to art quilts and everything in between.

Quilts and projects with many different fabrics are the most interesting and challenging to me. I can't seem to stop adding fabrics once I start, and sometimes other quilters have come to my rescue and lend me fabrics for even more variety. I have a number of different projects in progress at

15

any time, and find that a difficult spot in one project may spawn an idea or solution for another. I love the challenge of using fabrics to achieve special effects like depth, luminosity, and iridescence. I intend to focus more on original quilt designs and would like to publish patterns for my designs.

Inspiration and design

BUTTERFLY HOUSES was inspired by the two fabrics in the borders. While digging through my fabric stash for another project, I noted that the architectural print and the butterfly print were lying on the worktable together. I realized that the colors in the two fabrics were similar. The idea for a metamorphosis from buildings to butterflies was born. I hoped to create a scene in which butterfly houses were gradually transformed into butterflies.

To achieve the metamorphosis, I drew heavily on *Tessellations* by Jinny Beyer and, of course, M.C. Escher's many artistic works. I used the computer for much of the design process, using programs like *Tesselmania*, *CorelDraw*, and *Graph Paper Printer* for the tessellations and templates, and using the Internet to search for photos of tropical flowers for the garden.

The fabrics in the quilt are all cotton, and most of the pieces were cut by using templates or a rotary cutter. The quilt is machine pieced, except for a small amount of hand appliqué where the butterflies fly into the border. The flowers in the garden are paper-foundation pieced. The inner border fabrics were chosen to balance the colors used in the interior of the quilt. The pieced sections of the border connect one border fabric to the other.

All quilting was done on the machine, either hand or machine guided, with 30-wt. rayon thread in many different solid and variegated colors. The quilting designs were planned to enhance the scenic design of the quilt. Quilted butterflies dance in the air with curlicue breezes and shafts of sunlight. Details were added to the houses, plants, and

leaves to give definition to the garden, and water-like ripples and goldfish accent the fishpond. The butterflies were outline quilted in the ditch to accent but not overpower or obscure the design. The large border sections were quilted in a grid design, of either equilateral triangles or kites, to echo the lines of the quilt body.

Metamorphic design

The Tumbling Blocks quilt design is based on a hexagonal grid. The challenge, therefore, was to create the scene for BUTTERFLY HOUSES by using only shapes that could fit in the grid. For the houses, the hexagons are divided into two rhombus shapes, three diamonds, or six equilateral triangles, or a combination of shapes. In the fence, fishpond, and sky areas, the hexagon is divided into six equilateral triangles. For the garden, birds of paradise and other tropical flowers were drafted into triangle or diamond shapes for paper piecing.

The kite shape became the basis for the six-step transition from sky to butterflies. Using the computer program *Tesselmania*, I experimented to create a tessellating butterfly, beginning with various shapes that would fit into a hexagonal grid. By starting with a kite shape, I was able to create the most convincing butterfly image. Piecing lines were added to the final butterfly outline, as shown in Figure 1. Each hexagonal "tile" unit consists of six butterflies rotating around the center point where the tips of the front wings meet. Six different tile units were required to make the transition from the kite shape to the butterfly. A sketch on hexagonal grid paper became the map for the entire quilt design as it was created.

The architectural print in the lower-left border was cut and placed on the design wall first. Pieces for the houses were cut singly and placed on the wall so as to blend with the colors in the border to enhance the fade-in effect. Values are most important in the entire piece to achieve the three-dimensional effects and to make each butterfly separate

16

and distinct. Some of the houses are larger, made with the rhombus shape, and some are smaller, made with the traditional Tumbling Blocks pattern. The tropical flowers in the garden are paper pieced. The trellis fence is constructed with three different values, and large floral print fabrics were used between the fence pieces to look like flowers and foliage behind the fence.

The pieces for the butterflies were cut with templates and laid out on the design wall, starting at the right border and moving toward the center of the quilt. There are three different color combinations: orange, red, and green. All units have two light, two medium, and two dark butterflies. One

butterfly of each value is in the brown-gold-beige colorway. The units in the top-right corner are hand appliquéd over the outer border.

The sky and water pieces were filled in last. I wanted to achieve a misty look, very light, but with texture and depth. The open-frame inner border separates the body of the quilt from the pieced border sections. These border sections merge the two different border fabrics to create a softer transition.

Resource

Beyer, Jinny. *Designing Tessellations: The Secrets of Interlocking Patterns*. Contemporary Books, Chicago, 1999.

17

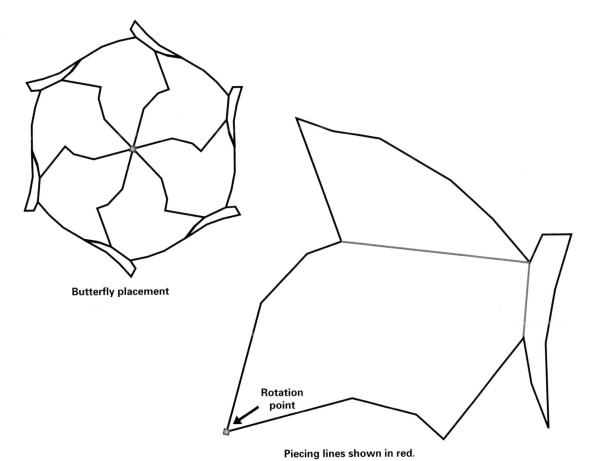

Butterfly placement

Rotation point

Piecing lines shown in red.

Fig. 1. Butterfly with piecing lines added in red.

Detail from BUTTERFLY HOUSES.

Tumbling Blocks: New Quilts from an Old Favorite

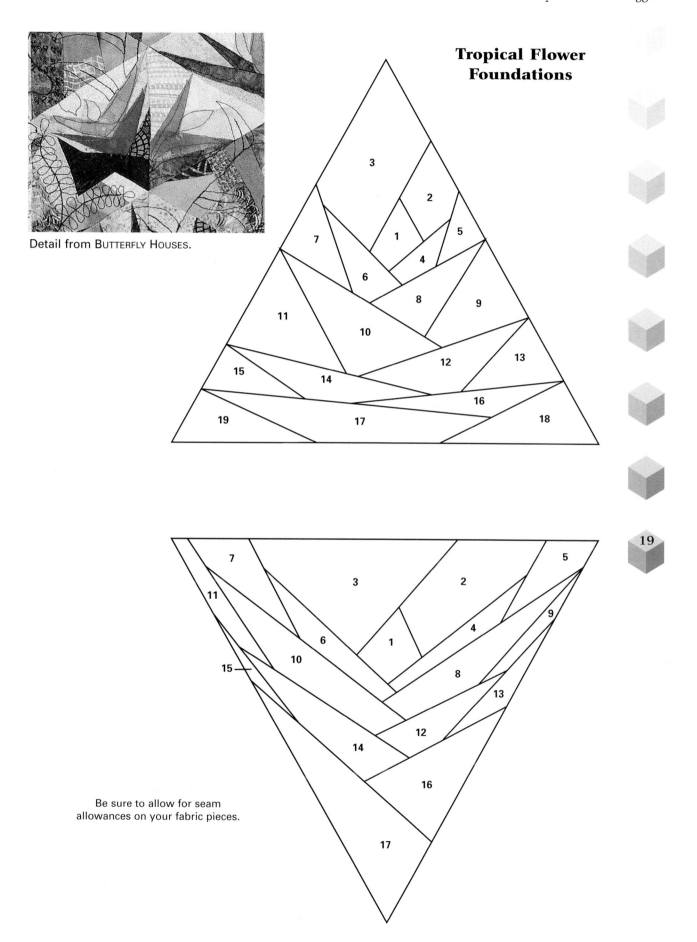

Detail from BUTTERFLY HOUSES.

Tropical Flower Foundations

Be sure to allow for seam allowances on your fabric pieces.

Tropical Flower
Foundations cont.

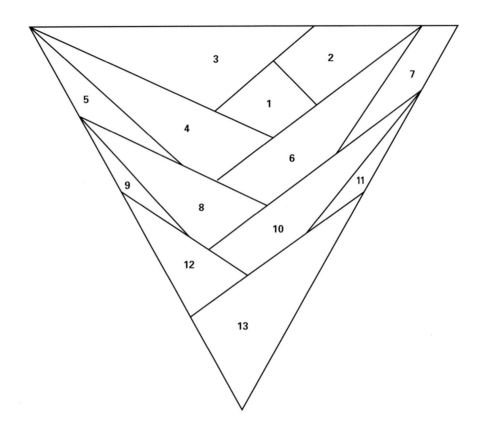

Be sure to allow for seam
allowances on your fabric pieces.

Detail from BUTTERFLY HOUSES.

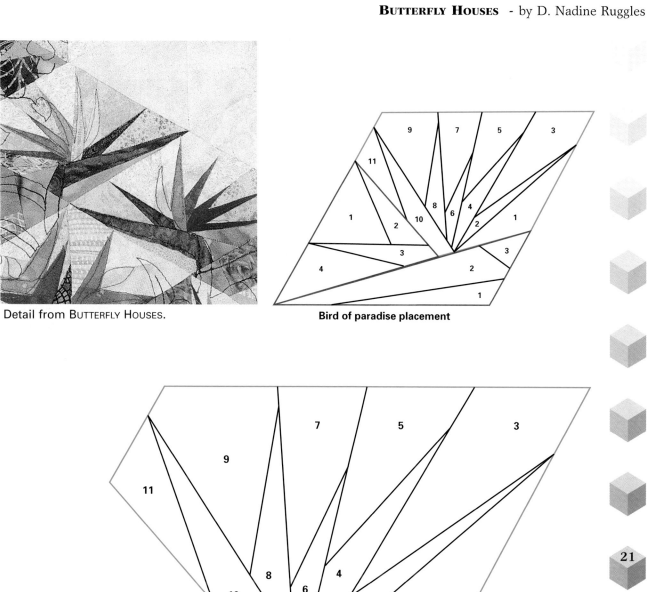

Detail from BUTTERFLY HOUSES.

Bird of paradise placement

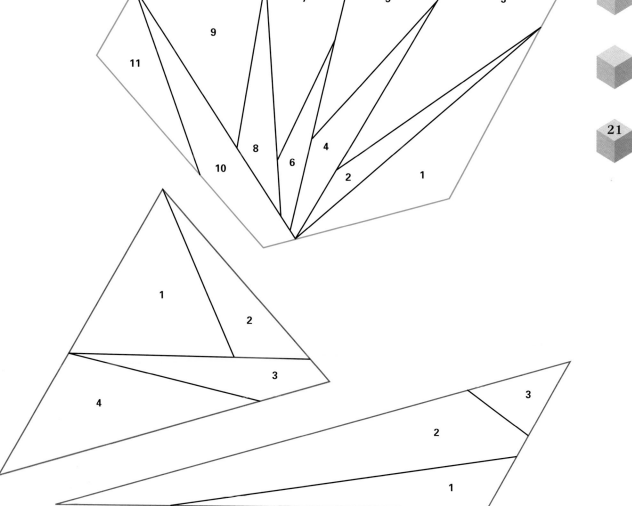

21

Tumbling
Texas Two Step

51" x 57"

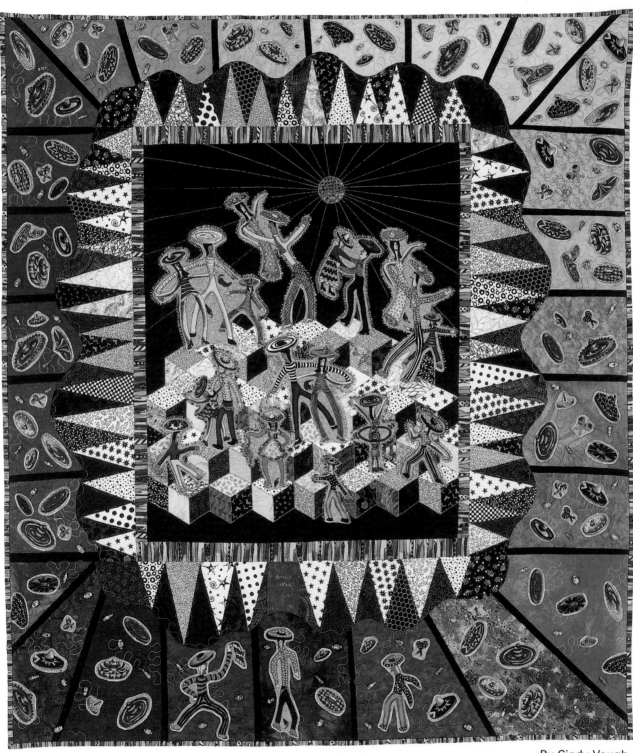

By Cindy Vough.

Tumbling Blocks: New Quilts from an Old Favorite

I TRY TO LEARN SOMETHING NEW WITH EACH QUILT, WHICH MAKES EACH PIECE SOMETHING LESS THAN PERFECT, BUT IT KEEPS ME INTERESTED IN THE PROCESS.

Nicholasville, Kentucky

Cindy Vough

Meet the quilter

I took a beginning quilting class about 22 years ago. It was not until my only child left for college and I retired from working as a cytogenetics technologist four years ago that I became a serious quilter. I have always sewn and, even with a scientific background, have loved art, color, and design. I gush over beautiful fabrics, and when I discovered the computerized sewing machine with its dependable thread tension, quilting became my passion. I sought out teachers who would expand my knowledge of the art of quilting and was so fortunate to be able to study with David Walker, Caryl Bryer Fallert, Aurturo Sandavol, Paula Nadelstern, Velda Newman, and many other experienced quilters.

I make quilts because they are always in my head, and I think about them until they become real. I love the challenge of doing something I have never done before. Frequently, this causes a lot of frustration when it doesn't work out the first couple attempts, but usually, I can keep trying until I come up with a solution to a problem. I try to learn something new with each quilt, which makes each piece something less than perfect, but it keeps me interested in the process.

My work is inspired by nature, fabrics (I work one day a week in a quilt store), other quilters' work, and art. My ultimate goal is to find a method of working or a style that is recognizable as my own unique approach to what is a wonderfully diverse medium. I do not believe I have achieved that goal yet and continue to try many different techniques. I am not drawn to traditional quilts but find that the traditional block can be a stimulus to producing interesting and exciting quilts.

This past year has been a successful one for me in quilting. Besides having a quilt selected for the *New Quilts from an Old Favorite* exhibit, I won first place ribbons at both the AQS and International Quilt Association shows. I was thrilled to have a piece accepted in each of those shows and was amazed to actually win something. The best part of quilting has been the wonderful people I have met and the dear friends I have made by actively participating in various quilting groups, both locally and statewide.

Inspiration and design

Tumbling Texas Two Step evolved over about six months, and although I had a general idea when it began, I did not know what the final product would look like. The creative concept for this quilt began in the sale rack of a distant quilt store. There I found three coordinating, funky fabrics that challenged me to think up a quilt to use them. I, of course, did not buy enough fabric, only a yard of each, but running out of fabric presented design opportunities.

Being aware of the Tumbling Blocks competition and needing a hand project to carry to quilting groups was the stimulus to make a dance floor of black and white Tumbling Blocks. My black and white fabric collection proved a fertile resource for the diamonds, which were roughly cut, then basted on commercially available paper pieces. One sleepless night, I arranged the pieces in what I hoped would look like steps or various levels of flooring. Then the pieces were joined by whip stitching them together.

I was not satisfied with the way the finished floor looked after hand assembly, so I decided to zigzag stitch over the seams with variegated thread in the machine. I also thought the project would be easier to handle if I made it in five parts, so the center of the quilt was made with backing and batting. The zigzag stitches in the floor also served as the quilting for that area.

The reflecting ball and rays were quilted before the figures were added. I did not fuse the figures because I do not always like the flat look that fusing produces, so I basted them on the center, then

machine appliquéd them with a satin stitch in variegated rayon thread. After the center of the quilt was completed, I added the bright narrow-striped border to both the front and back of the quilt. The outer borders were assembled and added to the center with batting and backing. The side borders were added first, then the top and bottom, then quilted with variegated thread in a meandering pattern. I was able to machine sew all the borders onto the center, but I had to slip stitch the striped inner border on the back to cover the seam.

Meanwhile, I came across a collection of Peruvian hand-painted beads, which I thought would be interesting in the border. I also thought that the figures needed something to make them sparkle, so I sewed several hundred bugle beads and at least as many multicolored glass beads around the figures. Because I had not used extensive beading in a quilt before, this was a new experience for me, and it kept me busy through many sewing bees.

Undulating spiky borders

This type of border is fun and easy to draw on paper for foundation piecing. The undulating line is done free-hand, or you can use any round or oval objects, such as plates or saucers, to draw it. You need only a ruler to draw the spikes.

I suggest you draw all the lines in pencil first to make sure the undulations and spikes come out even at the ends, then go over the lines in pen when your design is balanced and it suits your eye.

1. Starting with the side borders, cut two pieces of paper the exact length of the borders, excluding seam allowances, but at least an inch wider than the desired width.

2. Mark a dot at the same distance from the inside edge (toward the quilt) on both ends of the paper strips. These dots represent the start and

end of the undulating line. You want the measurement to be the same for all the borders, so the undulating lines will meet in the corners (Figure 2).

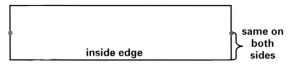

Fig. 2.
Mark the beginning and end of the undulating line.

3. Draw an undulating line at the desired border width. There's no need to try to make regular arcs or to make the borders look alike.

4. Using a ruler, fill the border with triangles, keeping them perpendicular to the inner border edge. Notice that the triangles are drawn all the way to the undulating line. Then cut along the undulating line (Figure 3).

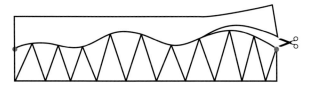

Fig. 3.
Cut along the undulating line.

Triangle Tips. The width of the spikes determines the look of the border and the amount of work required for piecing. If you have a lot of patience, you can make very narrow triangles, but I find that, if the triangles are at least 2" to 3" at the base, they are easier to piece.

5. Cut fabric strips at least ½" wider than the wide end of the triangles, then paper foundation piece the spikes. Trim the border, leaving ¼" of fabric around the outside of the paper pattern for a seam allowance.

6. Paper piece the top and bottom borders as you did the side borders. Be sure to match the ends of the undulating lines at the corners (Figure 4).

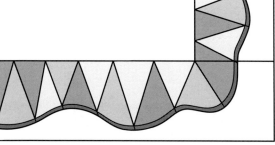

Fig. 4
Match the lines at the corners.

7. For each border strip, you will need a background rectangle the size of the undulating border. Then appliqué the undulating border to the rectangle (Figure 5).

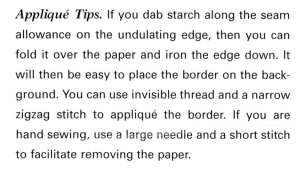

Fig. 5.
Appliqué the undulating border to the background.

8. You can now remove the paper and the excess fabric from the back of the border. Sew the undulating borders to the quilt as you would any butted border.

Appliqué Tips. If you dab starch along the seam allowance on the undulating edge, then you can fold it over the paper and iron the edge down. It will then be easy to place the border on the background. You can use invisible thread and a narrow zigzag stitch to appliqué the border. If you are hand sewing, use a large needle and a short stitch to facilitate removing the paper.

25

Quilter's Block

54" x 54"

By Nancy Cluts.

Tumbling Blocks: New Quilts from an Old Favorite

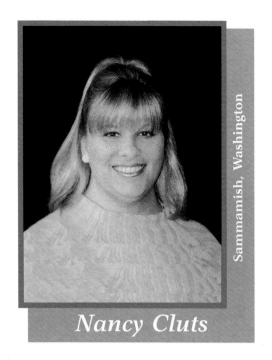

Sammamish, Washington

Nancy Cluts

OKAY, I DO
HATE BASTING,
BUT NOBODY
LIKES BASTING.

Meet the quilter

I started my first quilt more than 10 years ago, took my first class more than seven years ago, and have been an avid quilter for the last five years. I take classes and really enjoy learning new techniques. I like everything about quilting, from picking out the fabric to coming up with a design, actually creating the top, and then quilting it. Okay, I do hate basting, but nobody likes basting.

I create many quilts as gifts for family and friends and have made dozens of baby quilts in the last seven years, as well as many wedding gifts. The baby quilts are to be used. They need to end up tattered and fully loved, and I always promise that if the quilt gets destroyed, I will make another.

Lately, for each new quilt, I want to learn a new technique or a new way of looking at quilts. That means doing a lot of randomly curved piecing as well as working with low contrast, even though I'm a high contrast type of gal. I have also been trying hand appliqué in the form of Hawaiian quilting, as well as more daring thread play with all sorts of metallic threads and yarns. I also plan to try some layering techniques and fabric painting in the future. There is such a wealth of new things to try in the quilting world that I am sure I will never be bored.

Inspiration and design

The idea behind QUILTER'S BLOCK is a graphic representation of the quilter's equivalent to writer's block, what goes on in a quilter's mind when she is trying to create a new quilt and is stuck. I imagined a bunch of quilt blocks tumbling into a void. I created traditional quilt blocks of varying sizes and colors, placing the large blocks at the perimeter of the quilt and moving inward as the blocks got smaller (Figure 6). Once I settled on a pleasing arrangement, I needed to come up with a background. That was tricky. At first, I envisioned a dark background, perhaps emulating the universe.

27

But after previewing several different dark colors, I found that the darker blocks got lost in the quilt. Lighter backgrounds made the dark blocks stand out but made the light blocks fade. My solution was to use black and white strips in a pattern that created the optical illusion of falling inward.

The background was fairly simple to create with alternating strips of black and white, starting small at the center and growing by a half inch each time around the perimeter until I got the background to the desired size. The quilt blocks were then appliquéd on top of the background with invisible thread.

Fig. 6.
Nancy's original sketch on isometric perspective graph paper.

The traditional quilt blocks inside the tumbling blocks look deceptively easy to draw. They're just three-dimensional squares, right? But notice that the blocks are tilted to one side. This meant I couldn't use standard templates for the blocks.

Each block was first drafted on 30° isometric perspective graph paper to give me the angle for each block. After painstakingly creating a few of these, I realized that I could use some strip-piecing. I also decided to create my half-square triangles by the flip-and-sew method, which not only simplified the piecing but helped guard against stretching all those bias seams.

Once the quilt top was finished, I machine quilted the entire piece by first quilting the pieced portion of the blocks, then using invisible thread to echo the block onto the plain sides of each cube. In the background, I drew lines radiating from the center to the edges and used invisible thread on those lines to enforce the optical illusion of falling inward.

This was the most challenging quilt I have created to date. I learned so much while trying to figure out how to create the blocks: how to find an appropriate background, how to create an optical illusion, and finally, how to quilt a top and not detract from it.

Drafting tilted blocks

After creating my design, I knew it would be a challenge to draft the traditional quilt blocks. Luckily, I discovered isometric perspective graph paper online from a graph paper creator software program. This program allows you to set the angle to various degrees with varying sizes of diamonds.

Then came the task of drafting the blocks. I found the first one fairly challenging, but got the hang of it pretty quickly. I transferred the patterns to freezer paper to use as templates. After piecing together one block with the freezer paper method, I knew that this method would be tedious at best. At this point I realized that all that was needed was to cut strips of fabric and then cut the strips into skewed squares by using the 30° angle on my ruler.

Tumbling Blocks: New Quilts from an Old Favorite

For the half-square triangles, I found that it is easiest to put two squares together and sew diagonally from end to end. This method not only provided more accuracy, but more stability. By cutting the strips of fabric at different sizes, I was able to create the larger and smaller blocks needed to create the illusion of some blocks being farther away.

Tilted Block Patterns
(6" Blocks)

Churn Dash
6"

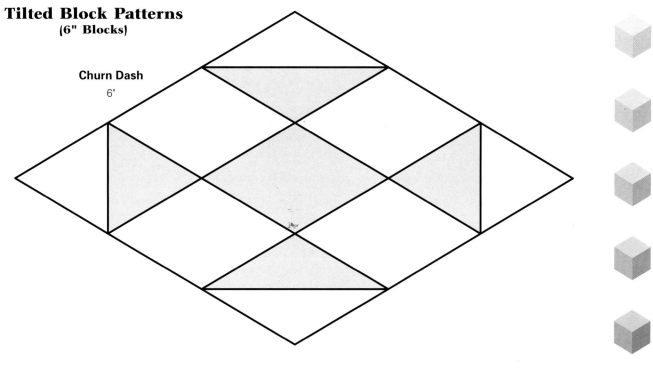

For more QUILTER'S BLOCK patterns, see pages 91-93.

Be sure to add ¼" seam allowances to your fabric pieces.

Sawtooth Star
6"

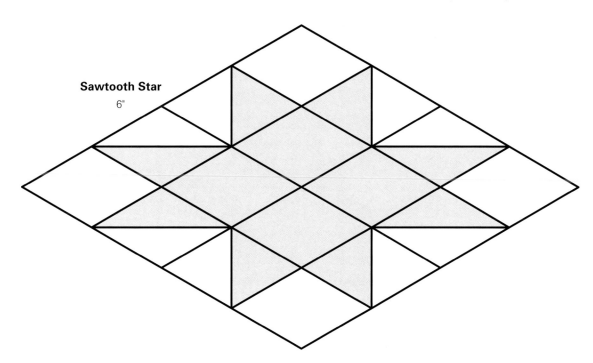

Tumbling Blocks: New Quilts from an Old Favorite

Glass Magic Blocks

50" x 53"

By Shelly Stokes.

Tumbling Blocks: New Quilts from an Old Favorite

Miltona, Minnesota

Shelly Stokes

I WELCOME NEW IDEAS AND CHALLENGES INTO MY WORK WHEREVER THEY APPEAR. THEY ALWAYS LEAD ME TO MORE ADVENTURES.

Meet the quilter

My adventures in quilting and fiber art began after a career in computer development and quality systems ended in 1995. The journey began with traditional quilting: bed quilts, lap quilts, and small wallhangings. I took up quilting as a way to fill my time and finally discovered the artistic medium I had been searching for – fabric. After learning the craft, I started exploring the realms of hand-dyed fabric and art quilts. I now own Cedar Canyon Textiles and sell my hand-dyed fabrics and fiber-related products at quilt shows and conferences in the upper Midwest.

I am currently creating two bodies of work. The first is called ROUGH AROUND THE EDGES. The pieces in this series are made with strips of torn fabric, and the raw edges are left on the surface of the quilts. The raw fabric edges are very much a reflection of the raw edges in my life, sometimes chaotic, sometimes orderly. I love the texture of these quilts. The edges provide a wonderful tactile counterpoint to the visual roughness of the torn fabric.

The second body of work is called GLASS MAGIC. This series is becoming more fiber art than quilt. It incorporates sheer fabrics and strings of dyed fabric to create a semi-transparent fabric resembling stained glass. GLASS MAGIC BLOCKS is the first quilt in the series to be made entirely from tulle (bridal netting) and cotton strings.

My fiber-art journey continues along several paths. I am learning the creation of art cloth in an independent study with Jane Dunnewold of San Antonio, Texas, to continue my explorations of color and texture in art quilts and other fiber art. I'm also building my business to include the sale of completed art work as well as fabric. In addition, I enjoy teaching other quilters and encouraging them to think outside the box and to expand their definitions of quilts. I welcome new ideas and challenges into my work wherever they appear. They always lead me to more adventures.

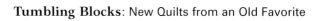

Inspiration and design

GLASS MAGIC BLOCKS is the most challenging quilt I have completed to date. The front and back of the quilt are tulle, and the filling consists of narrow strings of cotton. The result is a fabric that is partially transparent and has the look of stained glass.

Each of the diamonds in the blocks is an individual little quiltlet that was created and quilted before the assembly of the central medallion. The background was created in a single piece, and the center medallion was attached to the background by hand. Then the background was cut away from behind the medallion to reveal the back of the blocks.

After creating the border strips from more tulle and cotton strings, the background was slashed and the borders were inserted. All seam allowances are on top of the quilt. This construction essentially created a two-sided piece. The front of the quilt is fuzzy, almost like a rug because of the strings that hang out from the seam allowances of the blocks and the border strips. The back of the quilt has a more traditional, finished look. It is always interesting to see the reactions of the viewers. Some really like the texture of the front, and others prefer the back.

32

This quilt was challenging in a number of ways. The first challenge I set for myself. I had completed a much more traditional Tumbling Blocks quilt several years ago, and I wanted to create an artistic version of that quilt. The second challenge was more or less self-induced. Because of other commitments, I didn't begin working on this quilt until two weeks before the entry deadline. (My husband will tell you that I didn't do much else during those two weeks.)

The third challenge was the toughest. After viewing a quilt in which I had used some of my GLASS MAGIC fabric as inserts in a more traditional design, quilt artist and instructor Jane Sassaman challenged me to make an entire quilt from tulle and strings. She really pushed me to think about my work in a totally new way, and I am thrilled with the results.

In working with this type of non-traditional quilt, I have had to adjust my thinking about the need for my quilts to be perfectly flat and square. Because these fabrics are sheer, they simply don't have the body to stay perfectly flat, nor is it possible to add the traditional types of stabilizers that are often so helpful. I guess I just have to allow these quilts to be what they really are, more fiber art and less quilt. For now, the challenges have been met, and the process was a lot of fun. I wonder what would happen if I tried to make something really big.

Glass Magic technique

My adventures with GLASS MAGIC began as a recycling project. I had a bag full of fabric strings left from cutting my dyed fabrics into saleable pieces. The strings weren't nearly large enough to sew with, only about ⅛" to ¼" wide, but they were much too pretty to throw away. I had noticed an article in *Threads* magazine that explored creating your own fabric. So, off to the fabric store to buy a stash of tulle (bridal netting), and I was ready to roll.

Each piece of GLASS MAGIC fabric is a quilt in itself. The top and bottom layers are tulle, and the filling consists of strings of cotton or some other fabric. The trick is to get everything to hold together while you secure the layers with quilting.

In general, I use the following process:

1. Lay an old sheet on your work surface.

2. Cut two pieces of tulle to the desired size (about 5"x 7½" in GLASS MAGIC BLOCKS).

3. Smooth the bottom layer of tulle on the sheet.

4. Distribute the fabric strings in a pleasing manner and spray with basting spray.

5. Lay the top layer of tulle over the strings and press.

6. Carefully turn the three layers over so that they are bottom side up.

7. Lift the tulle off from the back and spray the back side with basting spray.

8. Replace the tulle and press.

9. Quilt as desired and trim the tulle to the shape of the quilting (Figures 7a and b).

10. Wash fabric to remove basting spray.

Fig. 7. (a)
The diamond shape is echoed in the quilting.

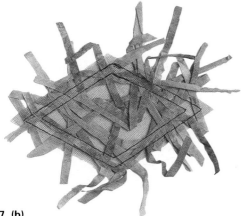

Fig. 7. (b)
Trim the tulle to the diamond shape.

For larger pieces, such as the background for the GLASS MAGIC BLOCKS quilt, I found that basting spray was not enough to hold the layers together during the quilting process. I had to pin baste the layers until they were quilted.

For smaller pieces of Glass Magic that I want to make in a specific shape, I find that freezer paper makes a great stabilizer. For GLASS MAGIC BLOCKS, I needed to make a lot of diamonds. In my early experiments, I found it difficult to work with small pieces of tulle. My solution was to cut rectangles of freezer paper to use as stabilizers. I cut a diamond from the center of the rectangles, then ironed them to the tulle before adding the strings inside the layers (Figure 8). The cutouts in the freezer paper made it easy to align the top and the bottom.

Fig. 8.
Freezer paper makes the pieces easier to handle.

I stitched a line ¼" from the edge of the template to secure the layers. I stitched a second line ¼" inside the first line to serve as the quilting within each diamond. Then I buried the thread ends as best I could within the layers and then cut away the tulle at the edge of the freezer paper templates. The result was a diamond of Glass Magic fabric with strings hanging out around the edges – just what I needed to create a fuzzy quilt.

The freezer-paper templates can be reused several times, but they eventually lose their ability to stick to the tulle. If you are going to make a large number of these shapes, it pays to make a plastic or cardboard template so that the resulting pieces are consistent in size.

The Day Our Stars Tumbled

55" x 61"

By Kathleen M. Andrews.

Tumbling Blocks: New Quilts from an Old Favorite

Kathleen M. Andrews

Rochester Hills, Michigan

QUILTING HAS NOW BECOME A STRONG BOND BETWEEN THE WOMEN IN MY FAMILY.

Meet the quilter

My mother and grandmothers taught me many of the needle arts when I was very young. About eight years ago, my sisters, Maureen and Colleen, who have been quilting for years, encouraged me to make a couple of small, traditional-style quilts. Quilting really didn't click with me though until my mom bought me a watercolor-quilt book and a fabric kit for Christmas one year. The quilt artist in me came alive, and I found quilting to be creative and satisfying.

Quilting has now become a strong bond between the women in my family. We all live in different states, so we try to get together at a different quilt show each year. When I go home, my face always hurts from the constant laughter. I am so lucky to have the support of my family. Even though she's not a quilter yet, my mom is with me for almost any quilt-related event. She's the best.

Inspiration and design

With a new quilt, I never have a full vision of what it will look like when finished. THE DAY OUR STARS TUMBLED was made in the same way all my designs are created. I make pieces and blocks and play with them on my design wall until there is a good layout. Photos of each layout help me remember what has been done previously. I then figure out the construction logistics, which is sometimes the toughest part because I don't like to do curved piecing or set-in seams.

This quilt was made during one of the worst times in U.S. history. It will forever contain tear stains from working on it during this terrible time. Tragedy came very close to our family because my brother-in-law was in the Pentagon at the time of the September 11th attack. We are so lucky he was able to get out. My heart goes out to all those who lost a loved one in this tragedy. In memory of all our fallen angels, I placed an angel in the center of each of the stars. God bless all our heroes!

Easy beginner's block

This block within a block is easy to strip piece, and there are no "Y" seams.

Cutting strips

You will need the following fabrics: light, medium, dark, and very dark for the background.

1. Cut two 2½"-wide strips from each of the light, medium, and dark fabrics.

2. Cut a 3½" wide strip from the very dark background fabric.

Sewing strip sets

Set A: Sew a light and a dark strip together. Press seam allowances toward the light strip.

Set B: Sew a light and a medium strip together. Press allowances toward the medium strip.

Set C: Sew a medium and a dark strip. Press allowances toward the dark strip.

Cutting strip sets

1. From tracing paper or template plastic, make a triangle template from the pattern on page 37. Include the center seam line on the template.

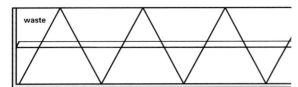

2. Layer Set B on top of Set C, right sides together. Following Figure 9, use the template to cut pairs of triangles. Be sure to align the seam line on the template with the seam line on the strip. For each block, you will need two pairs of triangles.

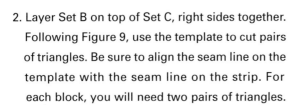

Fig. 9.
Cut layered strip sets B and C.

Cutting Tip: Do not separate the layered triangles. They are already paired for sewing.

3. Cut Set A in half and layer one half on top of the other, right sides together. Use the template to

cut triangles from the layered strip sets as before. Separate these split triangles into two groups by color placement.

Joining triangles

1. Sew the paired Set B and C triangles together, then add the Set A triangle to make half blocks, as shown in Figure 10. Press seam allowances toward the higher numbered piece.

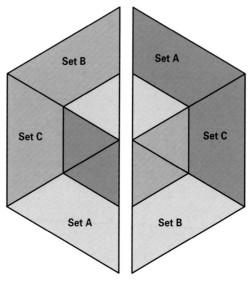

Fig. 10.
Sew triangles into half blocks.

2. Sew the halves together and press the seam allowances open.

Adding corner triangles

1. Cut the 3½" background strips into 6" rectangles. You will need two rectangles for each block.

2. Place one rectangle on top of the other, right sides together. Cut the rectangles in half diagonally. The resulting triangles are purposely cut oversized, so that after they are added to the block, you can trim the block to size.

3. Sew the triangles to the four corners of the completed hexagons. Trim the left and right sides of the block flush with hexagons. Trim the top and bottom by leaving ¼" seam allowances beyond the hexagon tips. The block should measure 8" x 9" (Figure 11).

Sewing Tip: To align the corner triangle with the split triangle, match the 60° corners.

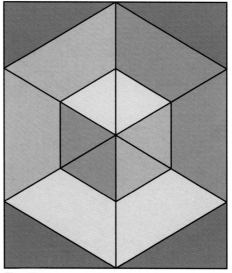

Fig. 11.
Add the corner triangles.

Beginner's Block Pattern

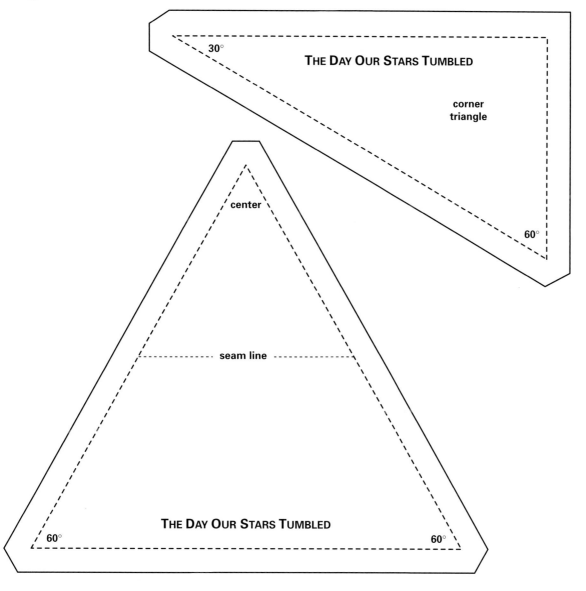

30°

THE DAY OUR STARS TUMBLED

corner
triangle

60°

center

seam line

THE DAY OUR STARS TUMBLED

60°   60°

Spin-Offs

70" x 81"

By Arleen Boyd.

Tumbling Blocks: New Quilts from an Old Favorite

Rochester, New York

Arleen Boyd

MY GRANDMOTHER, WHO LIVED WITH US UNTIL I WAS 7 YEARS OLD, TRIED TO TEACH ME TO SEW, BUT SHE ENDED UP SAYING, "ARLEEN, YOU WILL NEVER SEW."

Meet the quilter

My grandmother, who lived with us until I was 7 years old, tried to teach me to sew, but she ended up saying, "Arleen, you will never sew." My mother encouraged sewing and embroidery, which she did very well. She made all of my clothes and many for my dolls. She died when I was 12, and as a very naive girl, I assumed the only way to have clothes was to make them. Some projects were successful, but some went in the rag bag.

As a wife and mother, I sewed for our three girls and eventually started to teach sewing at home and in continuing-education classes. While visiting my husband's aunt, I saw her quilting in what I now know to be the quilt-as-you-go method. The ease of a small unit appealed to me. My first quilt was made that way, and kettle cloth was used for the backing. No wonder the quilting was slow going.

I needed instruction and signed up for Quilting II because Quilting I was filled. I had always sewn was my reasoning for jumping ahead. I soon learned that Quilting I was essential and took that next to catch up. Most of us in that class didn't want to stop quilting or getting together, so we formed a club, which is still meeting 20 years later.

Before discovering quilting, I took oil painting lessons. Because of that, I continue to have an interest in landscapes and seascapes and have made several quilts that depict scenes, some in the strip-pieced method, some with turned-under edges, and two with raw-edge piecing and free-motion quilting. With a folder full of scenic ideas, I hope to try more in that direction as well as stretching, bending, and distorting traditional blocks.

Quilting is both satisfying and challenging. The satisfaction of a quilt planned and completed just leads to new thoughts and ideas for the next one.

Inspiration and design

My quilt, SPIN-OFFS, is made from 100% cotton fabrics. Some are from my stash, but the medium background was purchased to pull the colors together and to provide a cool, contrasting color. The stars were cut in the Stack-n-Whack® method, and the ribbons were cut from 3½" strips with a 60° acrylic triangle ruler and a rotary cutter.

The idea for the quilt began as a result of a "mystery" class I was asked to teach. The project was a wallhanging with the Star of the East pattern, which has 60º and 120º angles. I had never worked with these angles but discovered they are versatile and have many design possibilities. I had already enjoyed using repeated designs in eight-pointed stars and had carried that over to the six-pointed stars. At that time, I selectively cut the star pieces and the woven ribbons, which were cut from a decorative stripe.

A while later, I made a large quilt with the basic Star of the East, and it was a dismal failure. The hexagons were too bright, and the stars too subtle. I discovered the error when the quilt was completely finished. I cut it up into place mats, table runners, wallhangings, and even potholders. The smaller pieces worked out okay.

40

The pattern still challenged me, and I wanted to make it work successfully. When the New Quilts from an Old Favorite contest listed Tumbling Blocks, I was ready to start a quilt for the contest. I rejected a block-by-block look and opted for a medallion with stars and blocks shooting out from the center. There are six Tumbling Blocks within the central design, and the quilt was assembled in six sections (Figure 12).

After the individual blocks were pieced and placed on my flannel wall, I pieced the quilt in six large segments to complete the construction. It was quilted at night while I listened to books on tape, a way to let the day run out pleasantly.

basic unit

Fig. 12.
The quilt is made in six sections.

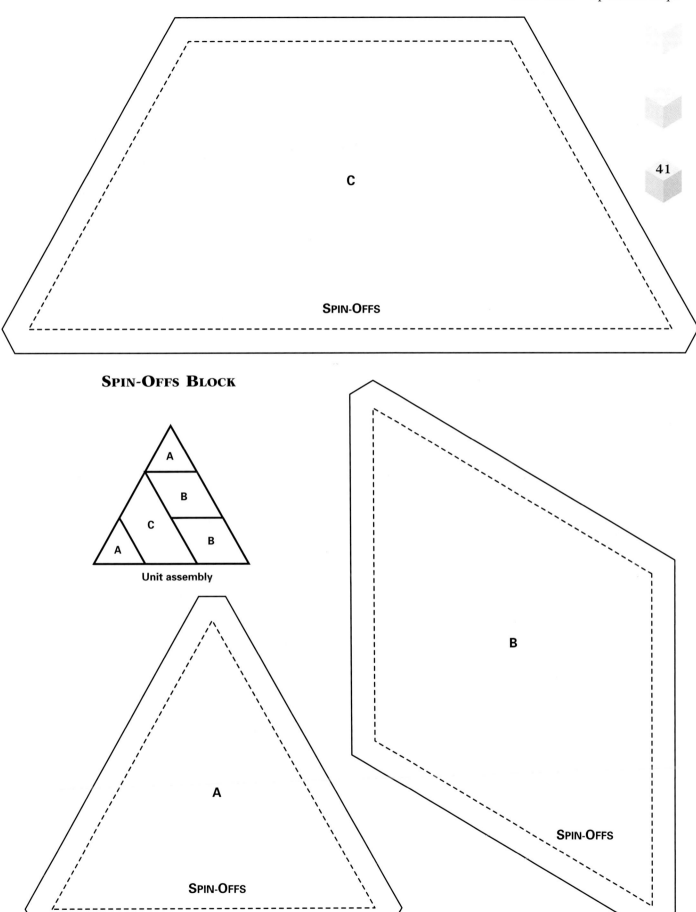

C

SPIN-OFFS

SPIN-OFFS BLOCK

A

B

C

B

A

B

Unit assembly

A

SPIN-OFFS

B

SPIN-OFFS

Tumbling Blocks: New Quilts from an Old Favorite

Blocks World

60" x 60"

By Lorrie Faith Cranor. Inspired by a Victor Vasarely painting.
Photo by permission of his daughter and heir, Michèle Vasarely.

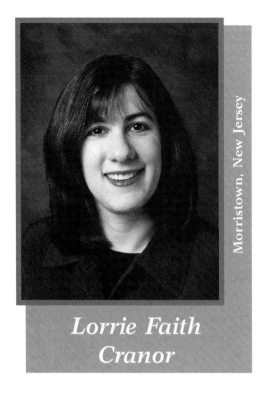

Morristown, New Jersey

I LIKE THE SERENDIPITOUS ASPECTS OF CREATING QUILTS OUT OF FOUND OBJECTS RATHER THAN USING FABRIC DYED TO EXACTLY THE RIGHT COLOR.

Lorrie Faith Cranor

Meet the quilter

I made my first quilt in 1993 as the *huppa* (canopy) for my wedding. The quilt depicted two swans swimming under a rainbow. I had no sewing machine, very little knowledge about how to make a quilt, and only a few weeks to complete the project before the wedding. I used a large rainbow cut from my brother's old bed sheets so as not to have to piece the rainbow, and I never actually quilted the quilt.

After the wedding, I bought some quilting books and made a series of small, hand-sewn wall-hangings and patchwork vests. As I worked on my doctoral dissertation, I often felt like I wasn't making much progress with it, but quilting was an activity that provided tangible results and a feeling of accomplishment. Unlike a lot of other artistic endeavors, such as oil painting, the mess I created could be vacuumed up easily. After finishing graduate school and getting a real job as a research scientist, I made my first major purchase, a sewing machine.

I had experimented with a lot of different art forms previously and minored in fine art in college. But when I discovered quilting, I felt I had finally found my medium. Most of my quilts are original designs that seem to have minds of their own. I often begin my quilting designs on the computer and pin a printout of my computer design to my design wall, but then I spend more time auditioning fabrics and rearranging my design than I do actually sewing. I find myself thinking and talking about what my quilts "want" as I create them. And I love to use many bright colors. I am still relatively new to quilting, and with a full-time job and a young baby, I haven't had time to make all that many quilts, so every quilt I make is a learning experience.

Inspiration and design

When the September 1998 issue of the computer science magazine *Communications of the ACM* arrived in my mailbox, the cover photograph of a Victor Vasarely painting immediately got me thinking about my next quilt project. I carried the magazine around in my briefcase for weeks, and in spare moments used Microsoft PowerPoint slide-making software on my laptop computer to reproduce the optical illusion, a stack of tumbling block shapes depicted in the painting. Once I had created a line drawing of the overall shape, I used my computer to experiment with different ways of coloring it in. In the original painting, the shape was composed of solid blue diamonds of various shades, each surrounding a smaller solid-red diamond. I introduced more colors by using a palette of blues, purples, and pinks. The small red diamonds in the painting provide a visual texture to the otherwise flat surfaces of the shape. I provided that texture with print fabrics instead and appliquéd smaller hot pink diamonds selectively, rather than onto every diamond. I also decided to let the shape of the block stack stand on its own, rather than set it in a fabric background.

While it certainly would have been possible to create a close replica of the original painting using hand-dyed fabrics, my goal was to use the painting as a starting point and interpret it as a quilt. I like the serendipitous aspects of creating quilts out of found objects (discovered by visiting lots of fabric stores!) rather than using fabric dyed to exactly the right color.

Once I had decided on the overall color scheme and the size of the diamonds, I began cutting diamonds from all of the blue and purple fabrics in my stash and placing them on my design wall. But I quickly decided that I didn't have nearly enough varieties of purple and blue fabric. It took me about three months to acquire enough different blue and purple fabrics to create the design, and then another three months to sew the diamonds together and complete the quilt. The final challenge I faced was applying the binding to a quilt with 24 corners.

Most of the fabrics I used are cotton quilting fabrics, but a few of the blue and purple diamonds are silk. The hot pink diamonds were first fused in place and then machine appliquéd with a satin stitch. I used a variegated metallic thread for the machine quilting.

Since I found the painting that inspired this quilt on the cover of a computer science magazine, I gave my quilt a name related to computer science. One of the first problems studied in many artificial intelligence classes is how to teach a robot how to rearrange a stack of blocks. This type of problem is referred to as a Blocks World problem. The quilt also makes me think of tall buildings in a city, with the hot pink diamonds representing the light coming from windows at night. This is a free floating city, made of nothing but blocks, sort of a science fiction planet, a Blocks World.

More of Lorrie's quilts can be seen on her website at http://lorrie.cranor.org/quilts/.

Square-Within-A-Square Block Pattern
(5½" block)

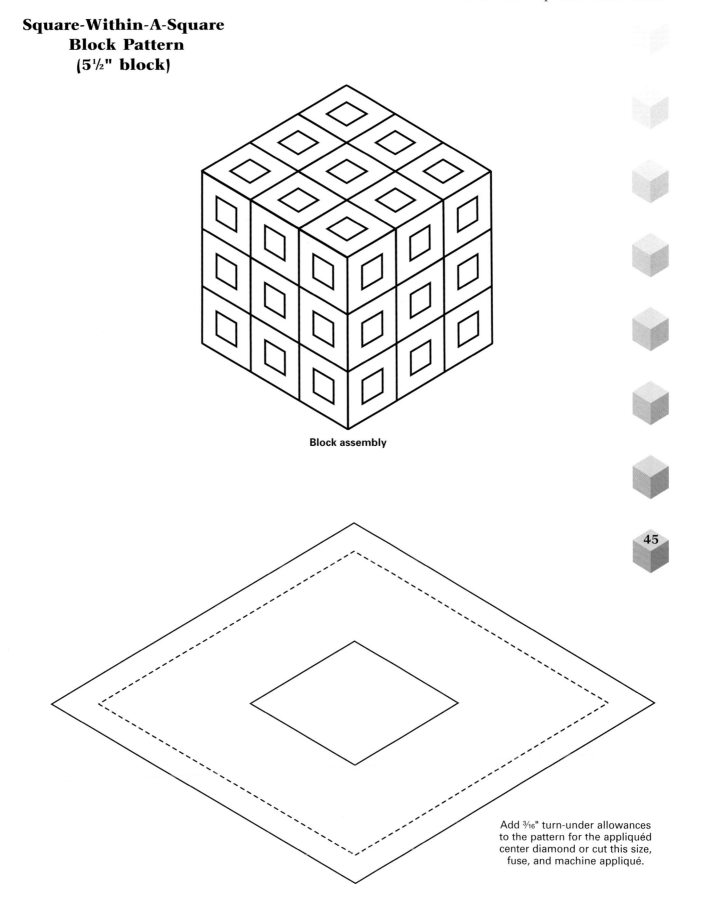

Block assembly

Add ³⁄₁₆" turn-under allowances to the pattern for the appliquéd center diamond or cut this size, fuse, and machine appliqué.

United We Stand

55" x 68"

By Patricia C. Dowling.

Tumbling Blocks: New Quilts from an Old Favorite

MY HUSBAND'S FIRST
RE-ENLISTMENT BONUS
WAS SPENT BUYING A
NEW SINGER ELECTRIC
SEWING MACHINE.

Calahan, Florida

Patricia C. Dowling

Meet the quilter

I started my first quilt in the 1950s, when my husband and I were both in the U.S. Air Force. While in my first tour of duty, we started a family, and I began sewing on an old treadle sewing machine for extra income.

My husband's first re-enlistment bonus was spent buying a new Singer electric sewing machine. I carried this machine along as we moved from base to base and sewed clothing for our two daughters. I also made quilts for our personal use. As our daughters started to school, I became a Girl Scout leader and taught the Scouts how to sew. The items we made were for local nursing homes, hospitals, and orphanages. When my girls were pre-teens in the 1970s, they helped me sew quilts as gifts for Christmas.

My husband spent more than 20 years in the Air Force, and as we moved, I began teaching new friends to sew. It wasn't until the 1980s that I had more time to design and complete more creative quilts. As our grandchildren came along, I taught my grandson and three granddaughters how to sew and make many quilts. In the early 1990s, I discovered that quilt competition was of great interest to me. I joined a quilting guild 40 miles away from my home, and I don't miss our monthly meetings because I enjoy sharing my ideas and learning from others. I have been fortunate to travel to AQS shows 11 years consecutively and return home energized and ready to begin new projects. I have many sewing machines and am always looking for new tools to make quilts faster and more professional. Someday, I would like to purchase a long-arm sewing machine, then I could finish the many quilt tops I have stored.

I am now a great-grandmother, and I hope to one day teach my great-granddaughter to enjoy sewing as much as I have enjoyed it over the years.

Inspiration and design

I enjoy every aspect of quilting, and sometimes the inspiration comes to me while I am sleeping. The design I chose for UNITED WE STAND is simple, and the fabric textures and colors do the work for me. There are so many wonderful textures and different fabric prints that my quilt expresses the message I want to relay. Creating the design began as a feeling from inside me. After choosing the fabric, I went to the drawing board and kept drawing until the basic idea was developed. At that point, I had to decide what the completed size would be.

I then named the colors I wanted to use. Like creating a plot in a story, silver was selected to represent the buildings. I had purchased this fabric without any idea for its eventual use, but the need to purchase it had been very strong. Red represents all the lives lost; black, the fears which were to come; and purple, the brave men and women who assisted in saving many lives. The white and black stripes represent the strength to recover and overcome the tragic events, and the dotted fabric stands for the many disruptions and insecurity felt by those of us who could only watch and hope for the best.

After I identified the fabrics to be used, then began the process of matching the shapes to the colors to develop the story I wanted to tell. Because black was to represent the fear of what was to come, this color was chosen for piecing the Tumbling Blocks. Purple was used in the simple squares above the towers. At this point, the quilt came together, and I knew where all the pieces would fit to sew my story. I began to feel better as I pieced my quilt.

I knew the quilt needed a special quilting design. The one chosen was a swirling distress design that could be free-form machine quilted in an inter-locking, never-ending flow. As I machine quilted on my portable sewing machine, I spent many hours bonding with this quilt, which compelled me to release the feelings I had held inside. I feel good about the expressions of my own creation, which is now to be shared with others. United we stand; God bless America.

48

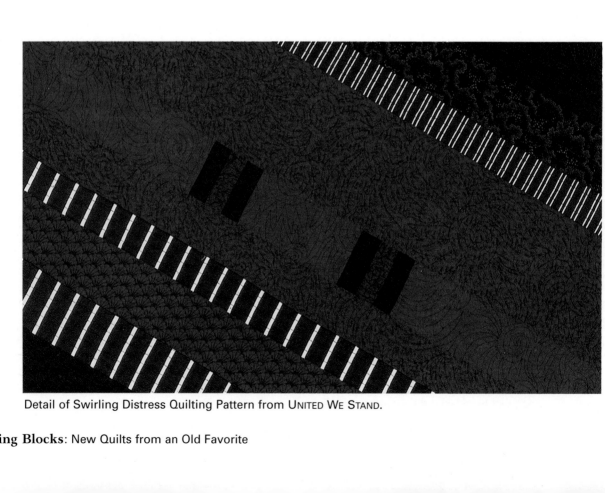

Detail of Swirling Distress Quilting Pattern from UNITED WE STAND.

Tumbling Blocks: New Quilts from an Old Favorite

Swirling Distress Quilting Pattern

Start

End

Rather than marking this continuous-line design, practice it at the size you need on a sample sandwich until you are comfortable with it. Then sew it free-hand on your quilt.

49

Everlasting Life

74" x 71"

By Yuki Fushiki.

Tumbling Blocks: New Quilts from an Old Favorite

> I AM VERY RESPECTFUL OF TRADITIONAL QUILTS. AT THE SAME TIME, I'D LIKE TO CONTINUE CHALLENGING MYSELF WITH NEW THEMES FOR QUILTED FABRIC ART.

Kawasaki, Japan

Yuki Fushiki

Meet the quilter

Twenty years ago, my mother-in-law was sewing patchwork. Her health being weak, I always went to the fabric shop for her. Then one day, after a quarrel with my family, I returned to the fabric store. I bought some pieces of cotton fabric for myself. It is hard to describe the happiness I felt in having made this purchase. At this point, I thought I should start sewing quilts.

During 1994, an American quilter asked me to join a round-robin challenge. This group consisted of highly skilled European and American quilters and myself, the only Asian member. While working with them, I encountered many differences. I felt there was a very high wall separating us, as I attempted to understand their words and actions. This experience made me stronger as a person.

Gradually, my children are becoming more independent. Sewing keeps me focused on something I enjoy. Therefore, I do not spend too much time dwelling on my children who are leaving home for their own lives. Now, I have more time to create fabric and patterns. I am very respectful of traditional quilts. At the same time, I'd like to continue challenging myself with new themes for quilted fabric art.

Inspiration and design

For many years, I had been considering making a quilt by using an original pattern, but like most housewives in Japan, I did not have the opportunity to study basic design. Fortunately, my desire for this knowledge became a reality when a few friends and I had the chance to join a patchwork design class taught by an American quilt artist. The teacher of the class helped me to discover my own abilities, and in the process, I felt something suddenly awaken in my mind. I found myself hungering for creative stimulation.

After mastering the development of tessellating patterns, I had a strong desire to make a quilt containing my original design as well as expressions of my innermost feelings. Life somehow flows among many events and many people, like tumbling blocks. I am one of the blocks amongst the many colors, each symbolic of something special. Red represents love, yellow is hope, green is bravery, and purple is myself. This color combination is not ordinarily used in my quilts. Because I could not find fabric I wanted for the background, I dyed fabric myself with onion skins. The quilting thread decorating this tapestry is a little bit of my life. When I finished, I felt fully satisfied. My life continues to tumble forward in an effort to become a more creative quiltmaker.

Translated designs

An equilateral triangle formed the foundation for my tessellated design.

1. A curved shape was cut from one side of the triangle and translated to one adjoining side.

2. From that side, a second curved shape was cut and attached to the side of the first cutout

(Figure 13). This tessellation method is called "translation."

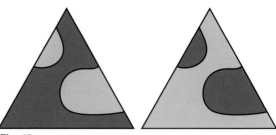

Fig. 13.
Translated triangles.

3. The altered triangle was rotated around a central axis to form a hexagon (Figure 14).

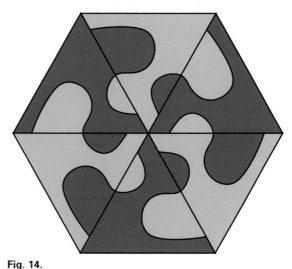

Fig. 14.
The completed block.

4. A combination of machine piecing and hand appliqué was used in the assembly of the pieces.

5. A series of hexagons were sewn together to make the quilt.

Close-up of translated triangles.

52

EVERLASTING LIFE
Block Pattern

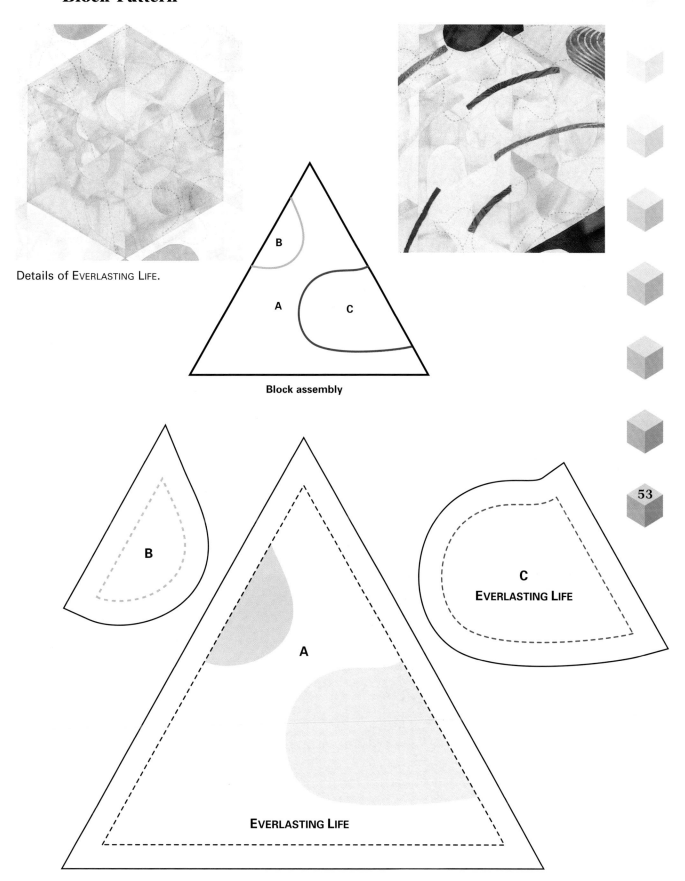

Details of EVERLASTING LIFE.

Block assembly

B

A

C

B

A

EVERLASTING LIFE

C
EVERLASTING LIFE

53

Block Party

51" x 51"

By Patricia Klem.

Tumbling Blocks: New Quilts from an Old Favorite

Rancho Sante Fe, California

Patricia Klem

I FIND IT EXCITING TO EXPERIMENT WITH THE RELATIONSHIPS BETWEEN COLORS AND THE CONSTRUCTION OF VARIOUS GEOMETRIC SHAPES, ESPECIALLY WITH LINES THAT ARE NOT STRAIGHT.

Meet the quilter

For as long as I can remember, I have enjoyed working with color and shapes, beginning with wooden blocks and Lincoln logs, beading, and sidewalk painting. However, at that time, a girl was encouraged to be practical, to become a nurse, teacher, secretary, or wife. So I became a home-economics teacher, taking all the college classes in clothing construction and textiles that were available. I learned couture sewing techniques, tailoring, and pattern design, and gained much satisfaction in making most of my clothes and, later, clothes for my children, friends, and anyone who would hold still long enough.

When I was introduced to quilting in 1975, a whole new world was opened for me. It was a way to combine my love of geometry with hand and machine sewing techniques. Quilting is definitely a tactile medium, and touch is an important factor in my life. I find it exciting to experiment with the relationships between colors and the construction of various geometric shapes, especially with lines that are not straight. In the past 10 years, I have been concentrating on original, contemporary designs. My quilts are conceived usually with pure design in mind as compared to those art pieces that make a statement or portray a realistic object. Sometimes I use the computer to plan a design, but there is always the element of surprise as the end result.

We all have the need within us to create. Some have it stronger than others and develop it in different ways: as an artist, scientist, chef, gardener, architect, mother, homemaker, mathematician, musician, etc. I believe that the process of creating is necessary for a fully realized existence. We get much satisfaction out of producing something where before there was nothing. Creativity for me also develops my spirituality and insight into myself and provides the opportunity to find new solutions and new, sensitive ways of observing my surroundings.

Tumbling Blocks: New Quilts from an Old Favorite

Inspiration and design

I have been experimenting with window-type designs in an architectural series in which color and value combined with piecing give the feeling of depth and layers. Templates have always driven me crazy. I'm more of a free-form designer, so I begin with a rectangular or square shape and then start cutting into it, adding strips over and under one another.

When Tumbling Blocks was announced for the theme of the competition, something clicked – a "eureka" moment – and I started making blocks in the window format. After piecing several sizes of blocks, I sewed the background and quilted it by machine. Then the blocks were arranged on top, and more were made and filled in, with attention to positive and negative spaces.

After only a short time, the quilt took on a life of its own, and I began to imagine that the blocks

were families living on the same street, having a block party on a pleasant summer afternoon. There were dad and mom blocks (the bigger ones) and teenager blocks (the medium-sized ones) and some small children. The blocks were ethnically diverse, of many different colors and designs, and as they visited with one another, they shared their favorite dishes of knishes, kabobs, tofu burgers, tamales, sushi, and other yummy specialties. Because of the sharing, all the blocks knew one another and respected their differences. Ah, well, so much for daydreaming. It just shows how this art form can transport me to another place. I love it!

Free-form blocks

You might like to try this easy, free-form method for constructing blocks:

Step A

Stash away the templates and free your mind. Begin with a square of fabric and cut it in half. Cut a strip to insert in the middle. In the samples, I

56

Step A

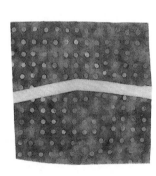

Step B

Step C

Step D

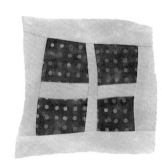

Step E

Step F

Tumbling Blocks: New Quilts from an Old Favorite

have used curved piecing, but if you are more comfortable with straight lines, use them.

Step B

Sew the center strip and the half-squares together. Notice that a contrasting value for the center strip will show up best.

Steps C and D

Cut the square in half the other direction and insert another center strip to make a "window."

Step E

Using the Log Cabin (Courthouse Steps) technique, add a window frame in a contrasting value.

Step F

Now comes the under-over part. Take a piece of fabric, about the same size as the window. Cut it in half and insert a center strip through it.

Steps G and H

Cut this piece into four strips to match the sides of the framed window and sew them on, trying to align the center strips so they look as if they continue across the square.

Step I

Add another frame and keep going as long as you like to complete the block.

Free-form variation

After completing Step E, cut through the window on each side of the center strip and insert two more strips (Step A). Then cut through the window on each side of the center strip, in the other direction this time, and insert more strips (Step B). Add a frame (Step C).

As you can see, this cutting, inserting, and connecting could go on for many layers, and when you have had enough of constructing windows, try connecting them to one another with a background of inserted strips. As you work, the inspiration will just happen. Have fun!

Step G   **Step H**   **Step I**

Free-form variation

Step A   **Step B**   **Step C**

Tumbling Blocks: New Quilts from an Old Favorite

Unwinding
56" x 61"

By Nancy Lambert.

Tumbling Blocks: New Quilts from an Old Favorite

Pittsburgh, Pennsylvania

Nancy Lambert

I ENJOY USING A WIDE VARIETY OF FABRICS AND COLORS AND WORKING WITH LARGER-SCALED PRINTS AND DESIGNS.

Meet the quilter

I had sewn clothes for a long time before I was introduced to quilting more than 20 years ago. At first, I made traditional quilts, all by hand. Then I began exploring more of the nontraditional avenues by using the sewing machine for piecing and appliqué and eventually machine quilting.

I enjoy the whole process of making quilts. I like taking a traditional pattern and making adjustments to it to give it another look. I also enjoy using a wide variety of fabrics and colors and working with larger-scale prints and designs. I like to push the envelope of what is expected, to give a quilt a new twist.

Inspiration and design

UNWINDING is made from 100-percent cotton fabrics, some of which were hand-dyed. The quilt top was machine pieced. I used a wide variety of color, mostly solids, but there are a few small prints included. I placed the colors in the quilt to show a progression over the color wheel.

I wanted to make a contemporary interpretation of the block, so I created many variations of the individual blocks and then of the overall pattern. I liked the feel of movement along the diagonal lines and took advantage of it by stretching and moving portions of the block. The overall pattern is still Tumbling Blocks. I added additional batting to some of the diamonds to create more dimension and some shading.

59

Large one-of-a-kind patterns

Here is the technique I use for making one-of-a-kind pieced tops.

1. Start by drawing a small design on paper; for example, a portion of the Tumbling Block design (Figure 15).

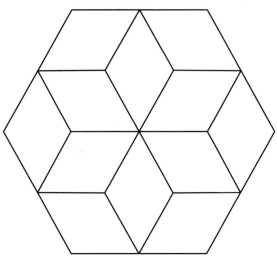

Fig. 15.

2. Modify the block by moving one or several of the internal points (Figure 16). Try variations by moving one point at a time. Once you find a drawing you like, enlarge it to the size you want.

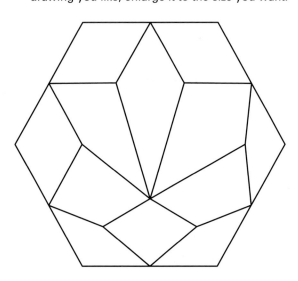

Fig. 16.

3. Use a photocopier and transparency film to make a transparent sheet of graph paper. Place the

transparent graph paper over the new design and tape the top edge (Figure 17).

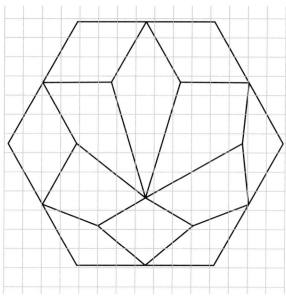

Fig. 17.

5. Make a paper copy of the design and the transparent graph paper over it.

6. Enlarge the paper copy to the desired size. On the enlarged copy, number each piece and indicate its color or value (Figure 18). This will be the master copy.

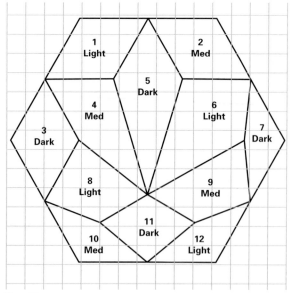

Fig. 18.

7. Make a copy of the master and cut out each of the templates from this copy.

Modified
Tumbling Block Pattern

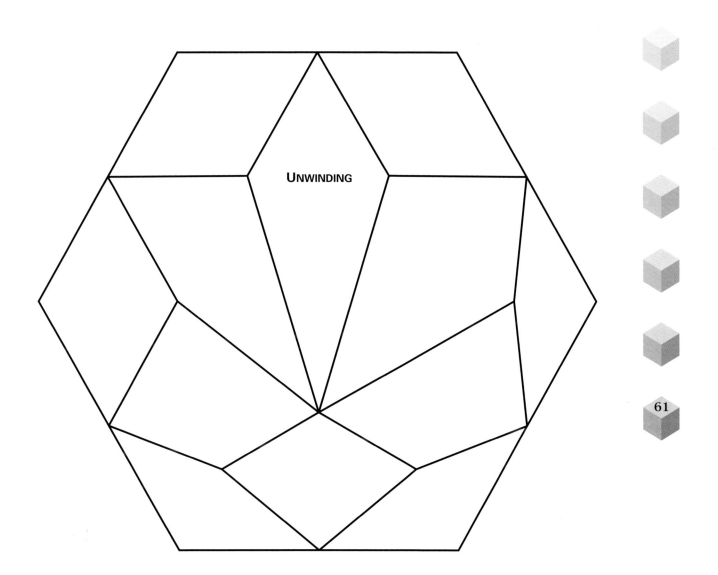

UNWINDING

Use this 6" pattern to make blocks for a quilt, or enlarge the pattern to use as the start of a large one-of-a-kind quilt or the center of a medallion-style quilt.

Be sure to add ¼" seam allowances to your fabric pieces.

61

Stumbling Blocks

52" x 71"

By Barbara Schneider.

Tumbling Blocks: New Quilts from an Old Favorite

MY BACKGROUND
IS IN VISUAL DESIGN, AND I
WORKED FOR MANY YEARS
AS A DESIGNER IN THE
PUBLISHING INDUSTRY.

Barbara Schneider

McHenry, Illinois

Meet the quilter

I began quilting in 1996 and rediscovered the pleasure of working with cloth, paint, dye, and thread. My background is in visual design, and I worked for many years as a designer in the publishing industry. I make handmade paper and collect Japanese folk art. I am working on a degree in ornamental horticulture and feel the need to connect with the natural environment every day. These areas of interest have had a strong influence on the development of my work.

My work has been selected for several exhibits in 2000 and 2001, including Quilt National, the World Quilt and Textile Exhibit, the American Quilter's Society Show, and the Yokohama Quilt Festival. My work is in several private collections throughout the country, and I teach workshops on surface design.

Inspiration and design

I decided to make this quilt because I have always liked the geometry of the Tumbling Blocks pattern. I like the fact that you can look at it and see different patterns emerge depending on the materials and orientation of the colors. A lot of my work is inspired by the Japanese concept of *Wabi-Sabi*, which is about finding beauty in things that are old, reused, or ephemeral. I see my quilt as another extension of that concept. I was able to use an old pattern in a new way, and I was able to use old and leftover pieces of fabric to create new fabric for the quilt.

63

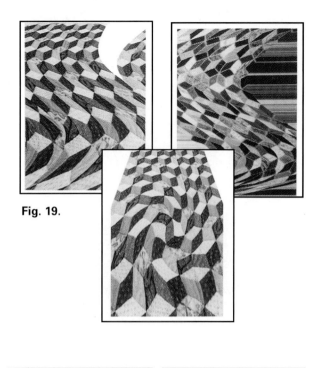

Fig. 19.

Computer design

When I started to create a new version of this old pattern, I worked with the concept on my computer by scanning an existing photo of a Tumbling Blocks quilt that I had made. I used Photo Deluxe, a photo program on a personal computer to manipulate the photo (Figure 19). I tried out many different alternatives. Some no longer read as Tumbling Blocks patterns, others would have made interesting quilts, only they were impossible to construct. I decided on a version in which the images spun outward from the center. I liked the movement that was created while retaining a recognizable Tumbling Blocks pattern.

I then worked on getting a version that was the right proportion with the right amount of spin. When I completed that, I printed it out on 8½" x 11" paper as shown in Figure 20, then traced the image as lines and marked the light, medium, and dark areas (Figure 21). The next step was to take the tracing to a photocopy center and enlarge it on their oversized copier. I split the image down the middle and enlarged each half to 24" wide and about 6 feet long (Figure 22). I then taped the pieces together and hung the full-size template on my design wall.

Fig. 20.   **Fig. 21.**

Making composite fabric

Then I had to decide how to assemble the quilt. I wanted the fabric choices to be fairly monochromatic so that the spinning pattern would remain strong. I determined that I liked the blue and white version best, but I did not like what was happening with using whole pieces of fabric for each of the block sides. I tried a number of solutions and arrived at cutting up all of my chosen

Fig. 22.

Tumbling Blocks: New Quilts from an Old Favorite

fabrics, which were primarily Japanese indigo and related cotton prints, into small pieces and then reassembling them crazy-quilt-style to make new fabric (Figure 23). I ironed fusible web onto the back of all the fabrics and then used a deckle blade in the rotary cutter to cut the fabrics into irregular widths. I cross-cut in the other direction, also in irregular widths. This gave me a lot of trapezoidal pieces. I used the backing sheet from a fusible web to reassemble the pieces. This allowed the fabric pieces to stick to one another but not to the sheet (Figure 24).

After I had several lengths of the reassembled fabric in dark, medium, and light values, I placed my full-sized template on the worktable, laid my white cotton fabric backing over it, and then used lightweight tracing paper to trace sections of the design, approximately nine to ten pieces at a time (Figure 25). I pinned the tracing paper patterns onto the composite fabric and cut a fabric piece very carefully, then placed the piece in position on the backing cloth (Figure 26). This was not a foolproof process! Adjustments and recuts were done and everything pinned in place. I then worked from the middle out and fused everything to the background fabric. After all the fusing was done, I squared up the quilt, added the inner red border, which overlaps the quilt center, and added the outer border.

I machine quilted with a variegated thread in medium blue to white. I let the various patterns in the fabric guide my machine quilting. I wanted it to be quilted quite closely so as to capture the edges of all the small pieces, but I did not want the stitching to change the overall perception of the spinning design.

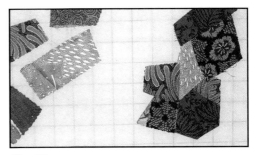

Fig. 23.

Fig. 24.

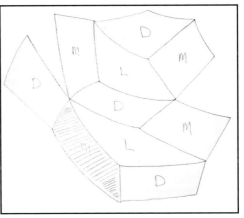

Fig. 25.

65

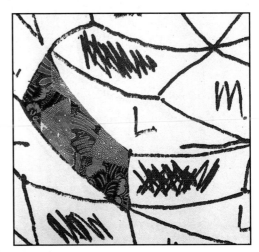

Fig. 26.

Earth Shattering
70" x 82"

By Lucy Silliman.

Tumbling Blocks: New Quilts from an Old Favorite

Fort Scott, Kansas

Lucy Silliman

MY QUILTS ARE
MADE TO CHALLENGE
MY INNER CREATIVE
SPIRIT AND, OFTEN, MY
DESIGN AND SEWING SKILLS

Meet the quilter

I began making quilts to commemorate my parents' and my husband's parents' fiftieth wedding anniversaries. My husband cut an article out of the newspaper about an anniversary quilt and said, "Wouldn't this be a great gift?" I had always made my own and my family's clothes but didn't have any idea about how to make a quilt. Armed with a new sewing machine and a lot of poly-blend fabrics, I completed the quilts, which are now family treasures.

Then I met some traditional quilters and learned to use a rotary cutter. I made traditional patterns until 1995 when I decided it was time to try my hand at my own designs. What a liberating experience! I gave myself permission that the quilt didn't have to match anything in my house. It didn't have to conform to anyone's expectations but my own.

Each quilt is now a new, exciting adventure. My quilts are made to challenge my inner creative spirit and, often, my design and sewing skills. Not having any background in the visual arts, I have tried to take classes and read books to learn the basic principles of design. Learning something new keeps my mind tuned-up. Hopefully, as I become a senior citizen, I will remain a vital, interesting person with forward-looking ideas. I don't have any time to get bored because there is always a new quilt calling to be made.

My work is mainly inspired by the colors that surround me in everyday life. I love pure, bright, clear colors. In fact, I have to be careful not to go overboard and to give the eye some rest. We are fortunate to live in an era in which we can find many vibrant fabrics. Inspiration has come from trips to other places and cultures. I usually try to buy fabrics as souvenirs and then combine them with photographs for new design ideas.

I also receive much inspiration from the fellowship with others who are open to experimenting with new ideas. I have recently joined the Kansas Art Quilters, a new group of fiber artists in my state, who are interested in forging new paths. It is exciting to see the many forms that fiber art is taking in the twenty-first century. I'm certain our ancestors would applaud our creativity as we carry on their tradition.

As for new directions, my favorite piece is always the next one. I'm spending more time now in the planning and drawing stage of a project, but I always want to leave room for serendipity. I want to "listen" to the fabric and let it "speak" and direct my creativity. I don't sell my work or do all the things an artist must to make a living; however, I don't consider my fiber art to be just a hobby. It is a compelling, vibrant part of my life that gives expression and vitality to my very being. It is art that gives a humanizing force of expression to all mankind.

Inspiration and design

The Tumbling Blocks pattern has always fascinated me because it has an interesting way of showing dimension on a flat surface. The use of value in this design creates astounding results, and the possibilities are endless. When I discovered that the blocks could be interlocked by placing an oval shape in the diamond, the possibilities increased dramatically. It became an intriguing challenge to see what new and exciting designs could be developed.

All aspects of a quilt should be interesting, so I began with a pieced background that could stand on its own. I wanted subtle changes in the texture while preserving a canvas to support the clear block colors. This part of the design was machine pieced and the border added.

The block portion was first built on my design wall with poster board shapes in black, gray, and white. I used my computer to enlarge the diamonds to

68

five different sizes to create the illusion of depth. When I had a pleasing design, I began to add the color. I machine pieced the blocks in a variety of colors and always tried to use one color family for each block. At this point, I simply played with the colors on my design board. I tried to use the rule that some colors come forward and others recede to give a greater feeling of depth.

After all the blocks were in place, I began slicing the ones that needed to go underneath. The entire design was basted in place, then hand appliquéd to the background. Because I do little hand sewing, this was the most challenging part. Straight lines in appliqué are especially challenging because they always seem to curve just a bit.

Finally, with the top completed, the pieces were layered with cotton batting and pinned for machine quilting. I stabilized the quilt by sewing around each diamond and each oval with invisible thread. Then, for the best fun – the free motion quilting – I used many different metallic threads to add just a little spice to the background. I tried to quilt down the background areas so that the blocks would pop forward.

I was inspired to make this quilt after coming to the Museum of the American Quilter's Society, as I do every spring when I attend the annual show in Paducah, Kentucky. It's an exhibit not to be missed! The quilts in the museum were at first intimidating in their mastery of design and workmanship, but as I progressed in my quiltmaking, it became one of my lifetime goals to have a piece of mine hang in this exceptional venue. I am very honored to be in the company of such outstanding artists as those that have been exhibited at MAQS. I believe the museum has been a major factor in the growth of quiltmaking, and it is responsible for catapulting fiber art into the explosion of popularity it now enjoys. MAQS is a tribute to past achievement and, through contests and classes, is a promoter of this truly American art form.

Interlocking Block Pattern
(10" block)

Use the pattern at the size given or enlarge or reduce as desired. Be sure to add allowances.

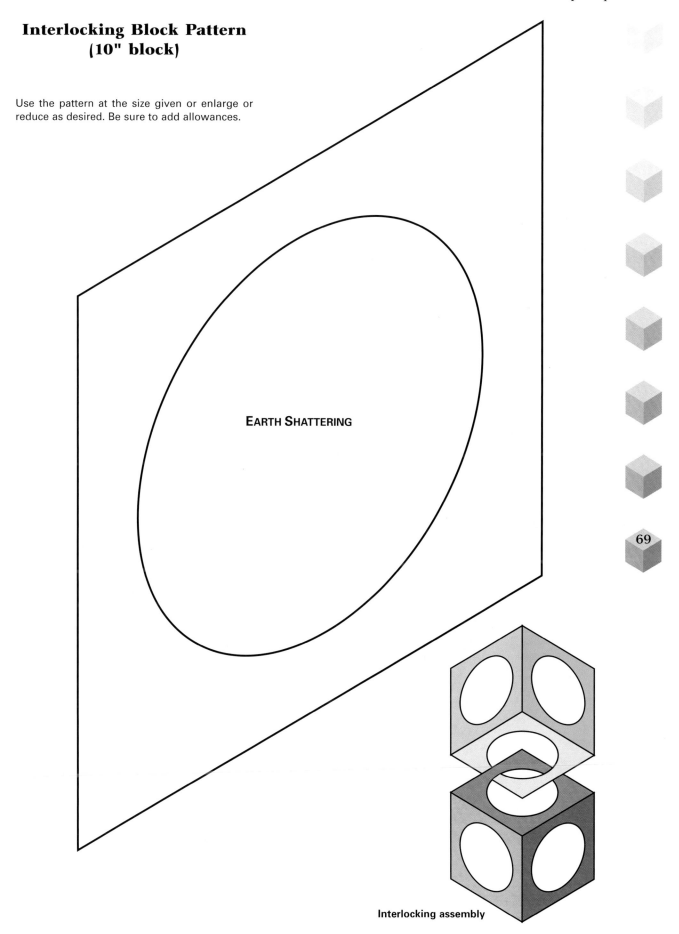

EARTH SHATTERING

69

Interlocking assembly

Tumbling Blocks: New Quilts from an Old Favorite

Tumbling Blocks

68" x 66"

By Janet Jo Smith.

Tumbling Blocks: New Quilts from an Old Favorite

> I AM STILL LOOKING FOR MY OWN INDIVIDUAL STYLE, BUT I LOVE TRYING IT ALL, INCLUDING FABRIC DYEING.

Morrison, Colorado

Janet Jo Smith

Meet the quilter

Over the years, I have worked with traditional patterns, played with innovative design, and studied numerous techniques with really terrific teachers. I am still looking for my own style, but I love trying it all, including fabric dyeing. Recently, I have moved back to traditional patterns, but with a twist. The MAQS contest provided the perfect opportunity to do just that and to explore the Tumbling Blocks pattern.

The future of my quiltmaking will probably continue with its roots in tradition. I like to experiment with low-contrast designs, by using contrasts other than value to create the pattern. I also like unusual color combinations. That, too, could be a theme. Now, if I only had more time.

Inspiration and design

While attending a quilt show recently, I saw the most unusual and wonderful batik fabric. I bought a yard, then went back to the booth and bought three more. I just couldn't resist the combination of chartreuse, blue-gray, turquoise, pink, and purple.

I searched my fabric stash at home for any pieces that would go with the batik, including calicoes, hand-dyed, stripes, and plaids, as well as other batiks. Because the pattern is based on diamonds and triangles, I cut hundreds of them in various sizes from all the fabrics. Then I began to play. The design started in the center. I wanted the viewer to see both a six-pointed star and a trio of blocks. Then the larger diamonds were pieced, and I arranged and rearranged them around the center until the design worked. By rotating the large blocks, turning them so the position of the darks and lights changed, the blocks appeared to be tumbling. The background batik was then cut to complete the top. Although it doesn't look possible, I used all four yards.

71

For me, this quilt represents a step back into quilt-making for exhibition after a three-year hiatus. It is a step back into my normal life, my quilter life. It is a huge honor and boost to be selected as a finalist in this competition.

Kindergarten design

TUMBLING BLOCKS was designed using a favorite technique of mine; that is, developing multiple units that fit together. In this quilt, I cut equilateral triangles and diamonds that, when sewn together, make a diamond the same size and shape as the larger patches. This method works best when done on a design wall. Like in art class in kindergarten, by using a flannel wall, you can choose your patches, arrange them, move them, and move them again until you have just the arrangement you like. After completing one of the large diamonds this way, you can start on the next. In making TUMBLING BLOCKS, I realized I was bored with all of the large diamonds constructed from small patches, so one diamond in each block is made using only medium-sized patches. It seemed that variety within this organized structure provided just the look I wanted.

This is a technique that can be used with any shape. Just divide the area into smaller pieces of the same shape. Figure 27 shows how this technique can be used with a Nine-Patch. The entire quilt is one large Nine-Patch block that has been divided and subdivided into smaller blocks. The outer row of the smallest units creates the border. The large center patch of the medallion provides an area for appliquéing a special design, or it too could be divided into an entirely different patchwork pattern.

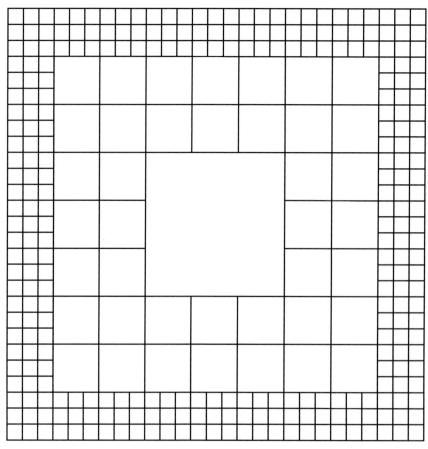

Fig. 27. Nine-Patch placement diagram of various sized blocks.

72

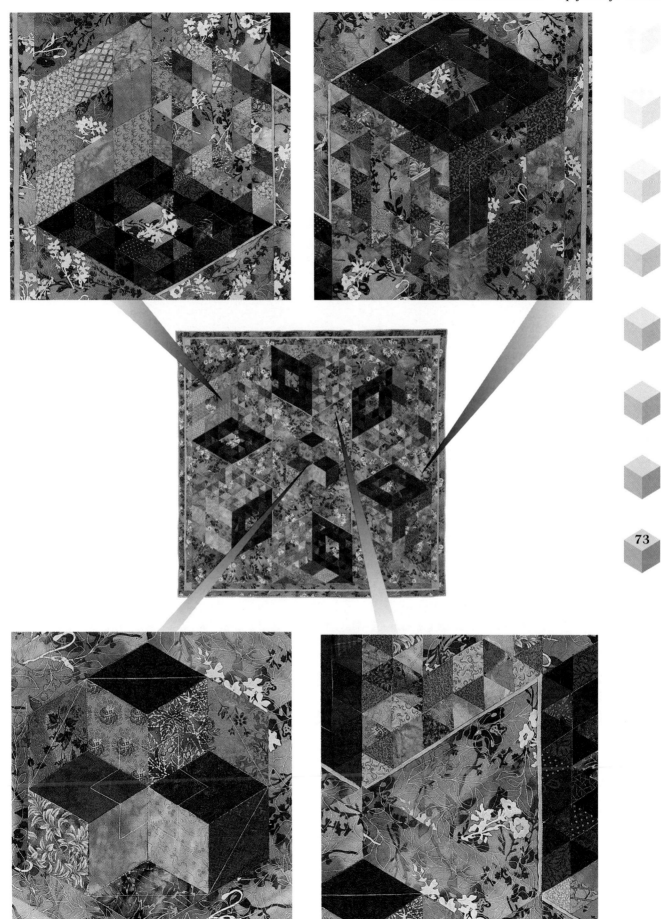

73

Tumbling Blocks: New Quilts from an Old Favorite

Let Freedom Ring

62" x 62"

By Judy Sogn.

Tumbling Blocks: New Quilts from an Old Favorite

Seattle, Washington

Judy Sogn

AFTER TRYING MY HAND
AT A LITTLE APPLIQUÉ HERE,
A LITTLE PIECING THERE,
AND EVEN A LITTLE HAND
QUILTING ON VARIOUS
PROJECTS, I DECIDED I COULD
PROBABLY MAKE A REAL QUILT.

Meet the quilter

I began quilting in 1982 with a lap-sized sampler, which was a Christmas gift for relatives. Before quilting, I had tried several hobbies, including knitting, clothing construction, and needlepoint. After trying my hand at a little appliqué here, a little piecing there, and even a little hand quilting on various projects, I decided I could probably make a real quilt utilizing all these skills. I was hooked from that moment on.

I remember being amazed at the wealth of possibilities in the quilting world. There were quilt guilds, local quilt shows, quilt shops, magazines, national symposiums, and contests. There didn't seem to be anything like that available to me with needlepoint. And even more amazingly, the opportunities have only continued to grow in the nearly 20 years I have been a quilter. I have always enjoyed the wide range of techniques that are included in the broader subject of quilting: piecing, appliqué, quilting, handwork, machine work, fabric dyeing, painting, printing, and surface embellishment. As quilters, we have a much greater choice of items we can make, from small quilted pincushions to clothing to large king-sized bed quilts. Just when I think there is nothing new to be discovered, some clever quilter comes along and proves me wrong with a wonderful new idea or technique. Better yet, she writes a wonderful book that I can add to my extensive collection, and who would have guessed that the computer would enter our quilting lives. It is a wonderful time to be a quilter.

Inspiration and design

Early in 2001, I designed LET FREEDOM RING by using the computer and quilting software. From the moment I started working on the design, the colors were set at red, white, and blue, probably because the design reminds me of patriotic bunting. I had finished the piecing and had just started quilting when the World Trade Center was attacked. Many hours passed as I quilted while watching the TV coverage of this terrible event.

Tumbling Blocks: New Quilts from an Old Favorite

Painless paper piecing

The arcs were pieced on just one freezer-paper foundation. For this technique, the paper is folded out of the way and you sew through the fabric only, using the fold as a guide. This method eliminates the need to tear the paper foundation away and saves paper, because the one paper template is recycled for all the blocks.

Foundation Patterns (10" block)

Be sure to add ¼" seam allowances to your fabric pieces.

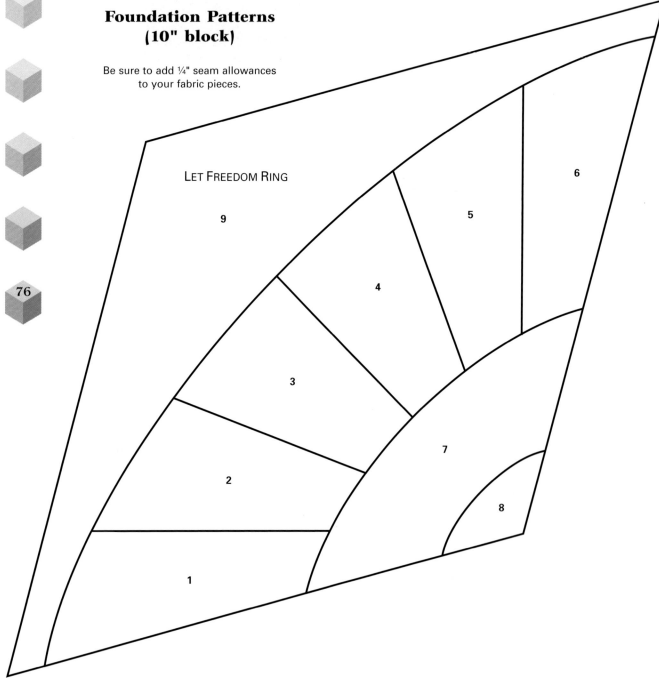

LET FREEDOM RING

9

6

5

4

3

7

2

8

1

76

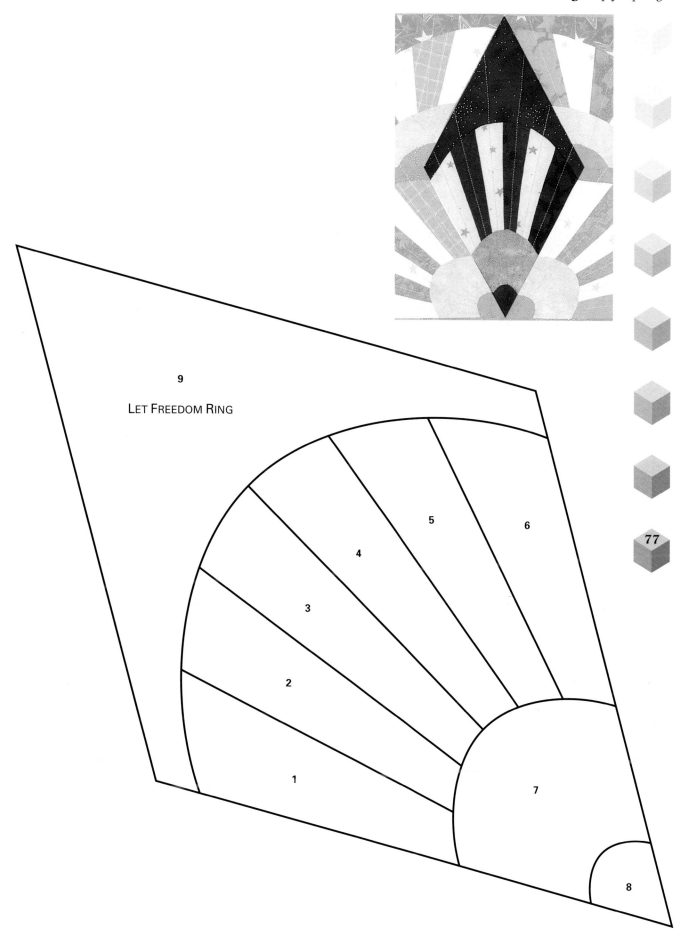

9

LET FREEDOM RING

1

2

3

4

5

6

7

8

77

Cats and Mice

100" x 82"

By Carolyn F. Tesar.

Tumbling Blocks: New Quilts from an Old Favorite

Portland, Oregon

Carolyn F. Tesar

T**HE WAY** I **MAKE QUILTS NOW DIFFERS A LOT FROM BACK THEN.** I **DO LESS PLANNING, ALLOW THINGS TO HAPPEN, AND WORK PROBLEMS OUT LATER.**

Meet the quilter

I made my first quilt in 1980, a large Crazy Quilt backed with Lemoyne stars. I had sewn clothes for myself for many years, so the fabrics came out of the scrap bag. They included cottons, flannels, knits, and denims. I didn't know anything about the proper way to quilt, so the stars were sewn with five-eighths inch seam allowances! It was a rough piece of work, but it is still being used.

I made a few more quilts during the next 10 years, learning new things as I went along. I got more serious after getting my own space for quilting. CATS AND MICE was designed with a computer quilting program. It was fun to manipulate the blocks and colors, so much easier than drawing on graph paper. As a novice user, however, there were aspects of the program that I missed, the most glaring being the finished size. I cut the strips for a finished width of one inch and proceeded with the quilt. It wasn't until the diamonds were being pieced that I realized just how big the quilt was going to be. I continued making blocks, but the quilt was overwhelming. It was obvious that my skills needed to improve before tackling this project again. It remained unfinished until the MAQS contest.

Over the next few years, I attempted many different types of quilts to learn new things: fabric challenges with friends, machine quilting as a design element, appliqué, etc. Because I am basically a self-taught quilter, this was a slow process. The way I make quilts now differs a lot from back then. I do less planning, allow things to happen, and work problems out later. This method grew out of my experience with the Tumbling Blocks leftovers. To practice the piecing, I took the extra strips and put them on my newly purchased design walls. I created two small quilts this way. One was a tightly structured piece in gray and black. The other had a more random layout and contained a full spectrum of colors. It was a turning point for me.

I can find inspiration from fabric as well as a topic. For instance, I like astronomy as a theme, having made two quilts about this subject, with another in the works. Another recently completed quilt tackled a more abstract concept as I explored color interactions, shapes, and textures on fabric.

I came to quilting for an artistic outlet because I had skills that I thought could be used in this medium. It feels wonderful to be able to express myself through my quilts effectively enough to be chosen as a finalist in this contest.

Inspiration and design

The dark gray variation in the light gray areas represents the darting and disappearing mice while they are pursued by yellow-eyed cats, represented by the yellow diamonds. The quilt was a collaboration between Pat Roche and myself. She took my concept and created a pattern of animals on the surface of the quilt, enhancing the original idea. The color scheme, and one of the cat outlines, came

from a particular fabric, which was the starting point for this quilt. It is one of a series of seven quilts.

CATS AND MICE has taken a long time to finish, having been unfinished for several years. Its large size, originally 120", and complex piecing delayed its completion. I always try to challenge myself, and as I grew as a quilter, the design evolved, resulting in what I now feel is a better piece.

This quilt doesn't contain any unusual construction methods. It is made of strip-pieced fabrics in the diamonds, which are joined into the hexagon-shaped blocks. When I made the strips, I pressed all the seam allowances toward the black stripe in the center of each small diamond. The large diamonds were more difficult to piece accurately because of this, but pinning carefully and having precise quarter-inch seams made it work. When it came time to assemble the blocks, I found it much easier to find the proper junction point if I pressed the seam allowances open. That way, the 120° angle is much easier to see, and it lies flatter.

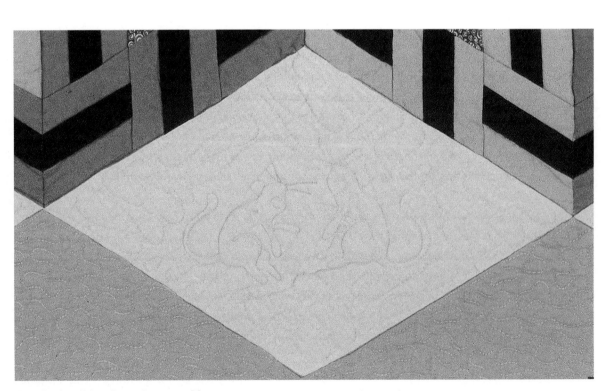

Detail of quilting from CATS AND MICE.

Detail of quilting from CATS AND MICE.

Detail of Tumbling Block from CATS AND MICE.

Stumbling Blocks

55" x 67"

By S. Cathryn Zeleny.

Tumbling Blocks: New Quilts from an Old Favorite

Napa, California

S. Cathryn Zeleny

I WAKE UP IN THE MORNING READY TO SEW. I FORGET TO COOK AND FORGET TO GO TO BED AS WELL, OFTEN STAYING UP UNTIL THE WEE HOURS OF THE MORNING TO FINISH SOME LAST BIT.

Meet the quilter

At a quilt show in July 1999, I purchased an eight-pack set of fat quarters in blue and white Japanese-style prints. Eleven days later, I had completed my first quilt. I designed it from scratch with 60 four-inch-square blocks, each made of 10 pieces, and all with curved seams, to portray an ocean wave. The quilting consisted of long sweeping lines and fan shapes. I should have been over-whelmed, instead I was hooked.

I have sewn since childhood, first clothing and then intricate stuffed calico animals, and I am quite proficient in piecing and handwork. I have since taken several classes in free-motion quilting, the major gap in my history with the needle arts. By trade, I am an artist and work primarily in colored pencil and acrylic paint, although I have experience in many mediums. I have also studied mechanical drafting and graphic illustration. Over the last 15 years, I have committed a significant portion of my time to the study of the design process and visual composition.

At the time of my introduction to the world of quilting, I was having a lot of difficulty finding meaning in my painting. I also missed the tactile sense of three-dimensional work and was considering ceramics. What a boon to make the switch to fabric. My hands get to touch and manipulate threads and soft cottons rather than wooden brush handles. I get to move from machine piecing to hand sewing and from playing with my stash to drafting a new design, rather than standing in front of an easel for hours on end. Even assembly-line chain piecing is a pleasure, especially when I am too tired to make important creative decisions. Today, it amazes me that it took me so long to discover quilting. It is the perfect blend for my technical expertise and my desire to produce aesthetic visual images to share with the world.

83

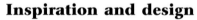

I have been creative since early childhood, but this is the first time in my life I feel that what I am doing is a calling. I wake up in the morning ready to sew. I forget to cook and forget to go to bed as well, often staying up until the wee hours of the morning to finish some last bit. If it weren't for my husband's patience and his willingness to vacuum, we would be starving while knee-deep in thread and scraps.

Most of the pieces I create are abstract art quilts or pictorials, with strong diagonal movement. They are either vertical or square in format. I choose colors that are bright and true and rely heavily on value change to create interest. My preferred fabrics are commercial cottons with patterns that are either marbled, geometric, or abstract. I use a lot of small, intricate machine piecing to produce the foundation of the quilt, which I then enhance with hand-appliquéd details or organic forms. My quilting pattern is usually a haphazard, free-motion zigzag. In just two years, a personal style has emerged which, while rooted in my painting preferences, still allows me to experiment with the wonderful diversity that quiltmaking offers.

84

Inspiration and design

In my in-depth studies of design, I have formulated some truths about the creative process. These are not like the rules of composition, which are merely guidelines that are intentionally broken in the modern art world. Instead, my design truisms are critical for my success.

My favorite is "tell one story at a time." It means that a single idea most readily communicates to the viewer the intent of the artist. In conjunction with this is "choose the compositional elements that support and enhance the story, while remaining subordinate to it." Every line, shape, color, texture, etc., should be chosen as the best representative of the central theme of the work. The third related truth is "create enough alternatives that you have choices between good and better." Do not rely on your first inclination, nor on habit. Always generate more options than you need. My

quilt, STUMBLING BLOCKS, was created specifically for the MAQS competition. It is intended to be a tongue-in-cheek metaphor for the obstacles in life's path, and it was the third of more than 40 completely different ideas that I considered developing (Figure 28a and b).

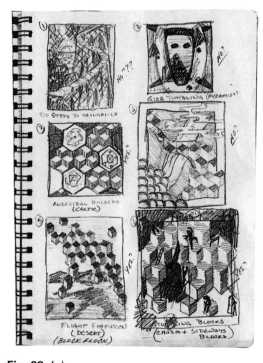

Fig. 28. (a)
A page from Cathryn's sketch book for STUMBLING BLOCKS.

To support my central theme, I used a lot of compositional elements that enhance the apparent difficulty in climbing up the blocks, in overcoming our trials. A vertical rectangle was chosen as the format. The blocks form a pyramid, which creates visually dynamic diagonal lines. The border goes behind the blocks, leaving the illusion that they continue. The blocks themselves have been modified from the traditional pattern, so that it appears we are below the horizon line, looking toward the top. Even the colors I chose, black on one side and black and white on the other, cause a visual line where this dramatic value change takes place. Our eyes accept the unity of the block while still being forced upward.

At the top, an "Under Construction" sign stops the viewer from going off the edge, bringing us back in to look at the blocks in the sky and the red-

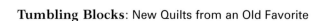

Fig. 28. (b)
Final working sketch.

Changing horizons

The traditional Tumbling Block can be modified to portray a higher or lower horizon by moving the center point up or down on the center vertical line. Lines A, B, and C will always remain parallel to each other and will have the same angle from the vertical center line and both side lines. I chose 20° for the angle, which moves the horizon above our eye level. To continue the illusion, the vertical edges of the box are made longer than the top and bottom edges (Figure 29).

orange climbing man. He and his cohorts are the details that not only provide humor, but also give us a sense of real place. This is further enhanced by the choice of organic, curved pieces in the sky and chasm, and by the ladders and signs. There is even a little red-cross station. I played down some compositional elements so that they do not compete with the visual image of the block pyramid. Color was kept simple, and the patterns in the fabrics are small and unobtrusive. There is little texture from surface embellishment or quilting.

I continued to generate design alternatives throughout the entire construction process. The man holding the detour-sign chain was a late addition. The door at the bottom was moved several times, and it wasn't until the very end that I chose my free-motion zigzag quilting pattern as the best representation of the chaos inherent in life's difficulties.

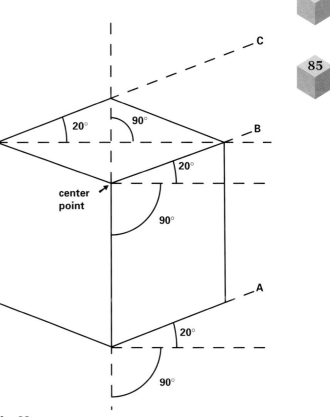

Fig. 29.
Horizon above eye level.

STUMBLING BLOCKS Pattern
(20°horizon, 5" block)

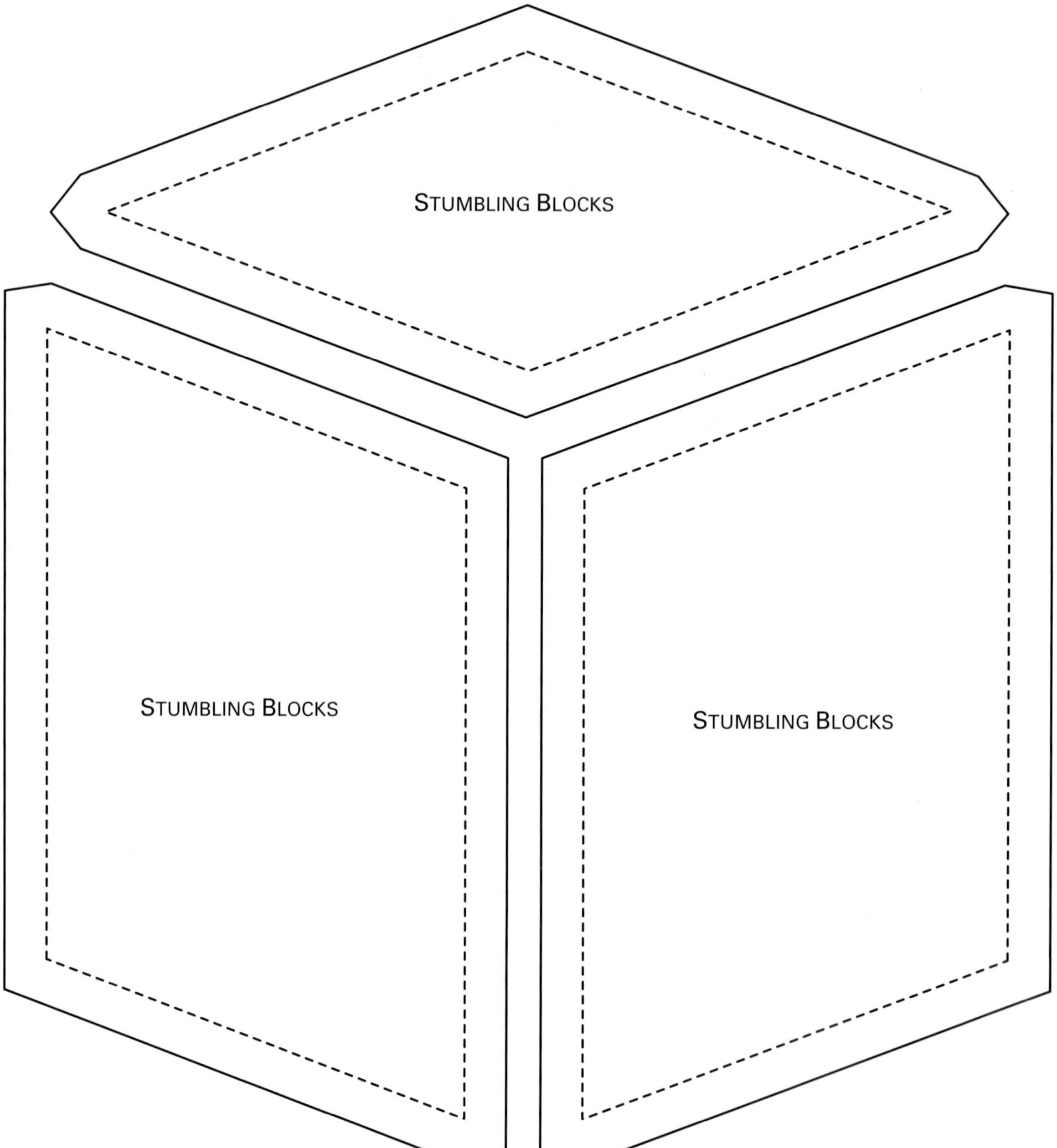

STUMBLING BLOCKS

86

STUMBLING BLOCKS

STUMBLING BLOCKS

More Tumbling Blocks Patterns

We have included full-sized template patterns for several sizes of basic Tumbling Blocks. Additional blocks from QUILTER'S BLOCK, page 26, are on pages 91-93.

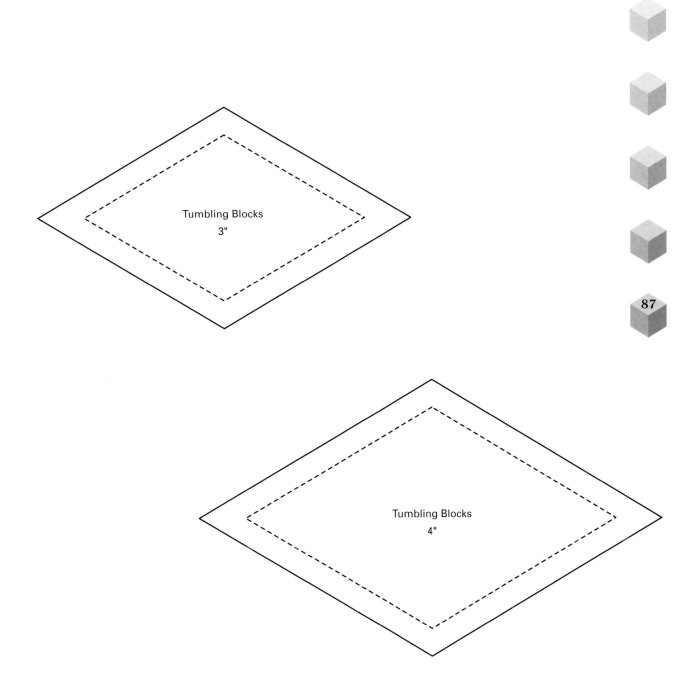

Tumbling Blocks
3"

Tumbling Blocks
4"

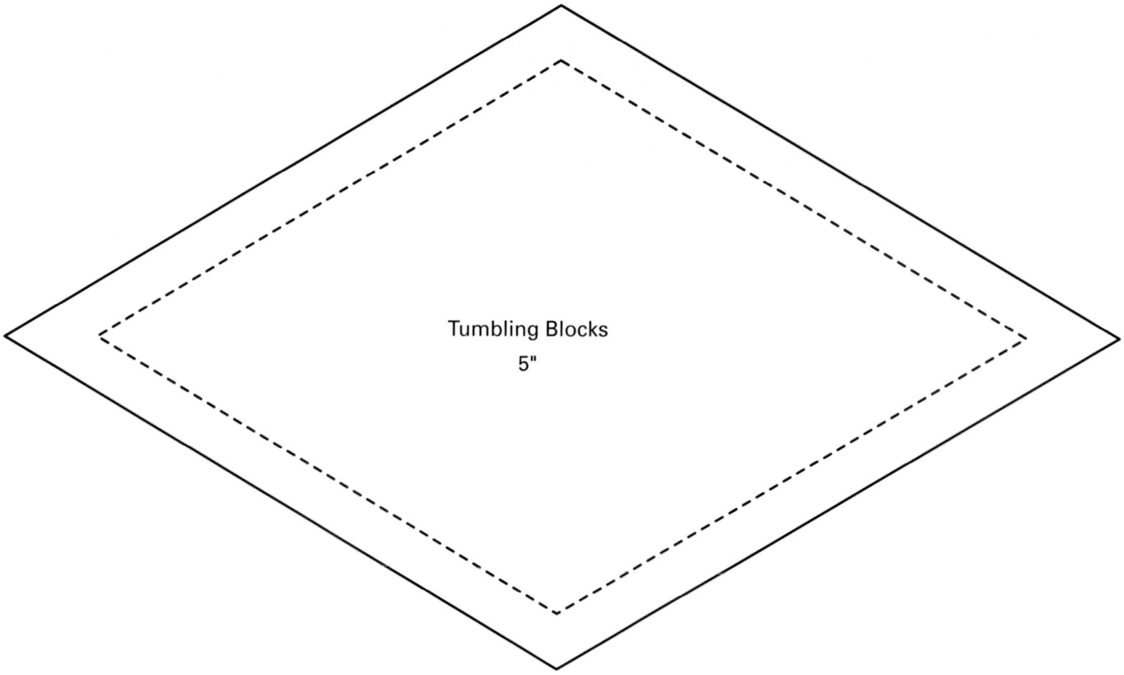

Tumbling Blocks
5"

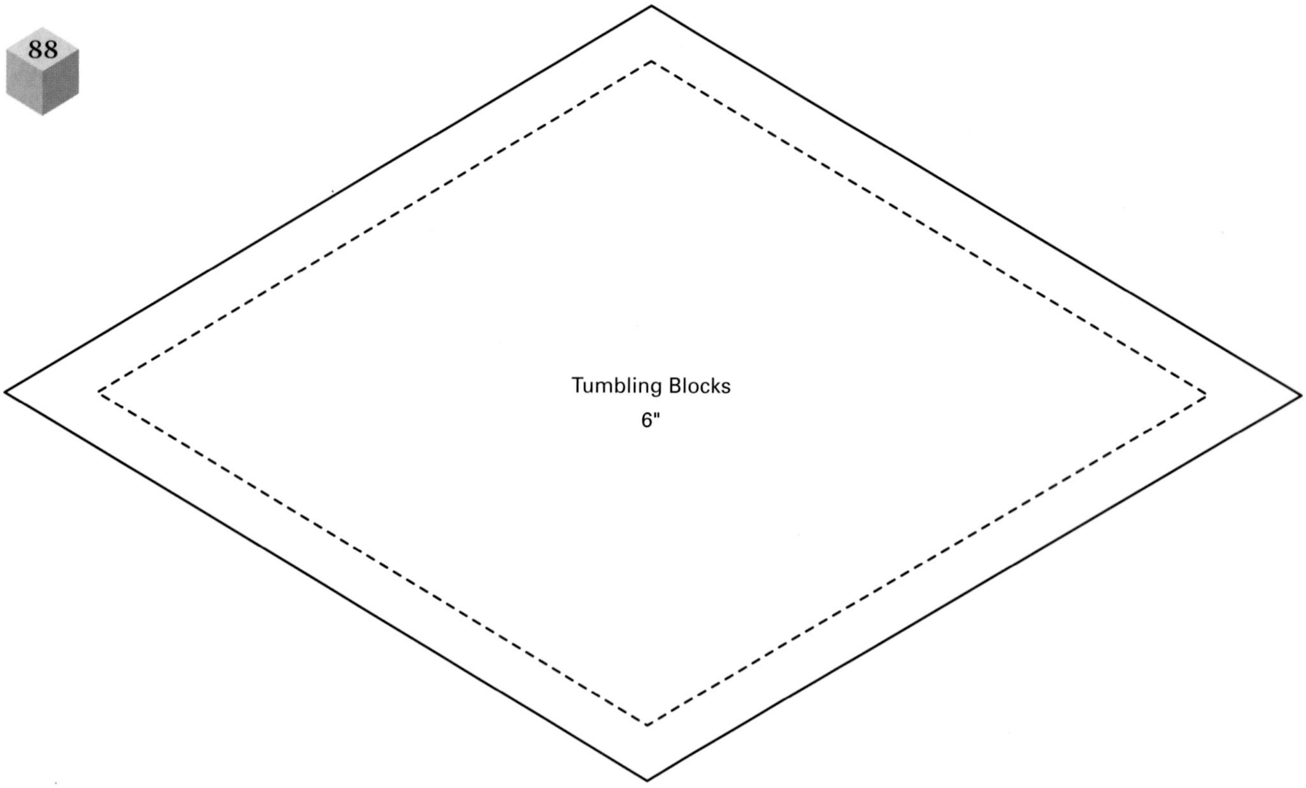

88

Tumbling Blocks
6"

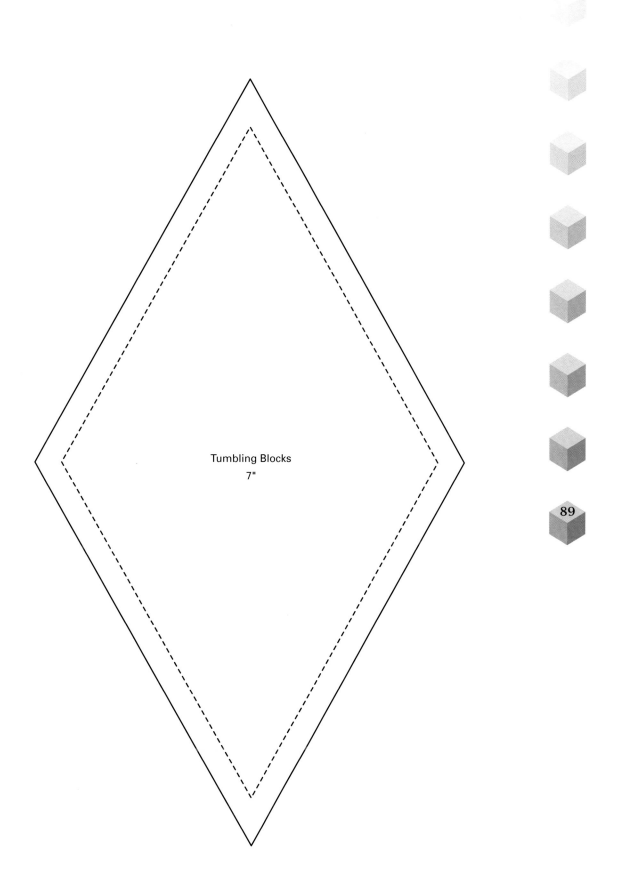

Tumbling Blocks
7"

89

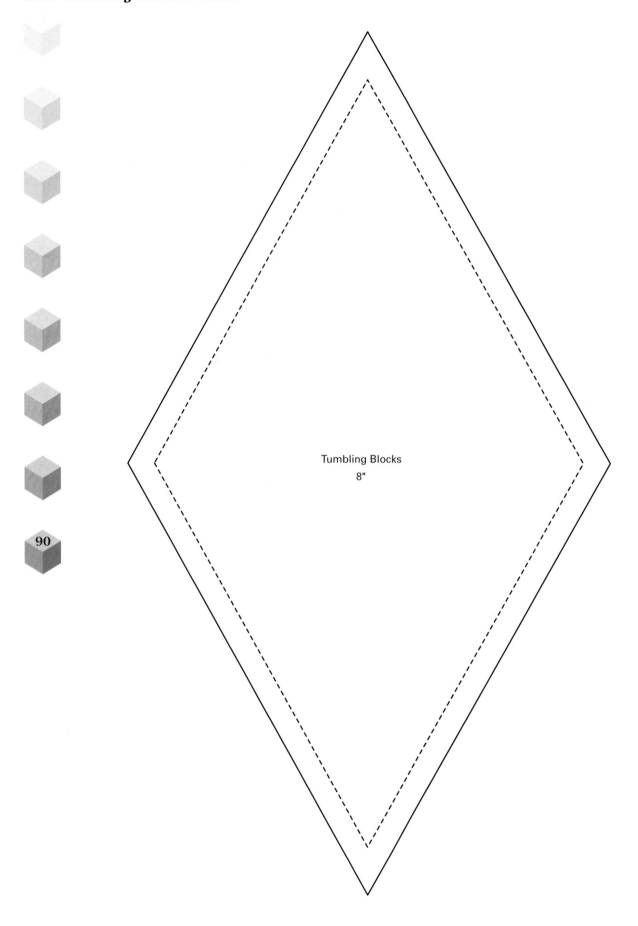

Tumbling Blocks
8"

90

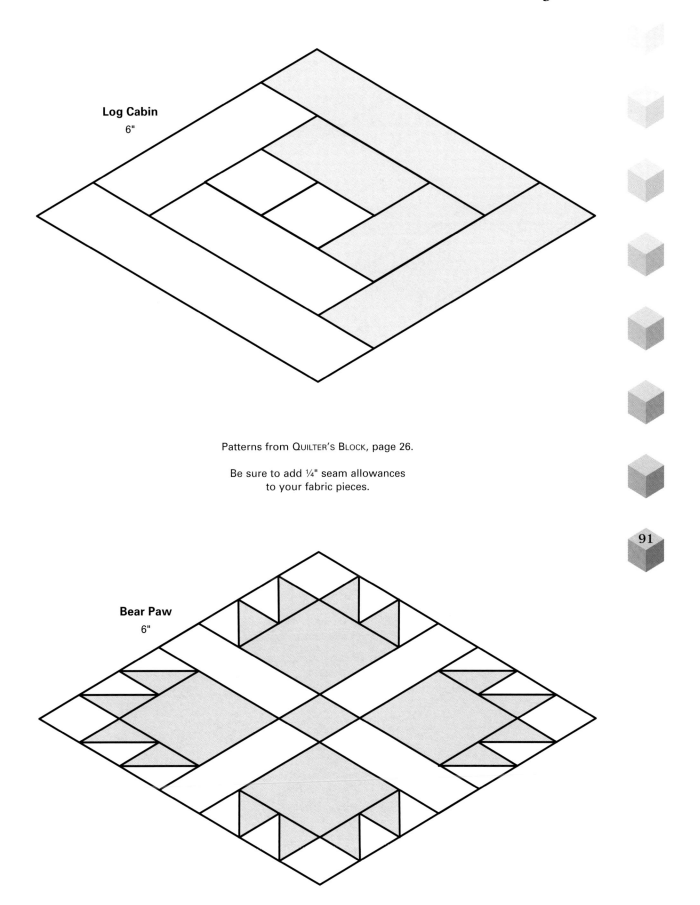

Log Cabin
6"

Patterns from QUILTER'S BLOCK, page 26.

Be sure to add ¼" seam allowances
to your fabric pieces.

Bear Paw
6"

91

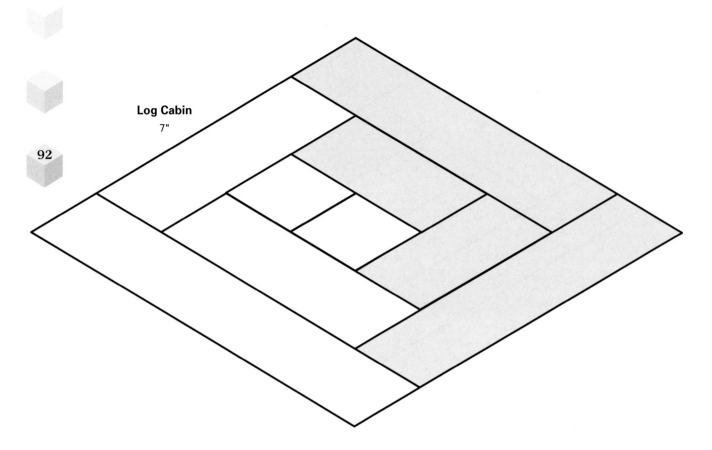

Log Cabin
7"

Patterns from QUILTER'S BLOCK, page 26.

Be sure to add ¼" seam allowances
to your fabric pieces.

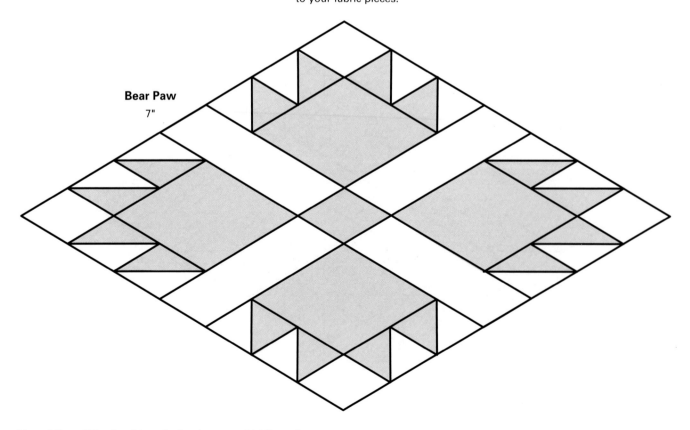

Bear Paw
7"

Tumbling Blocks: New Quilts from an Old Favorite

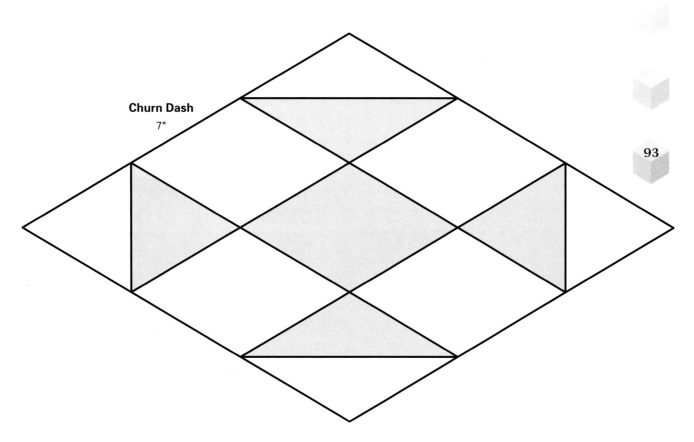

Churn Dash
7"

Patterns from QUILTER'S BLOCK, page 26.

Be sure to add ¼" seam allowances
to your fabric pieces.

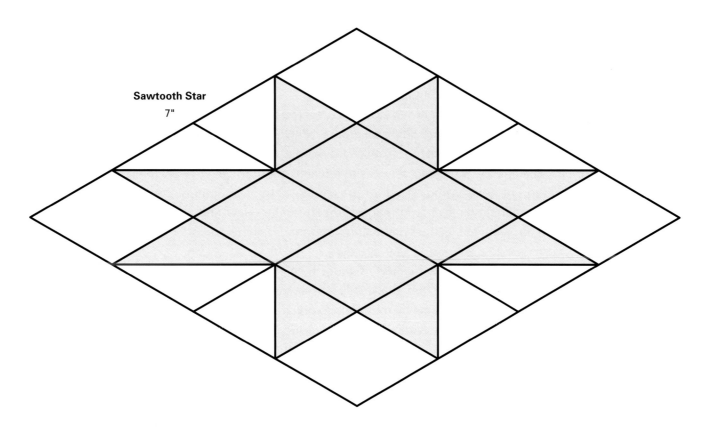

Sawtooth Star
7"

The Museum

The Museum of the American Quilter's Society (MAQS) is an exciting place where the public can learn more about quilts, quiltmaking, and quiltmakers. Founded in 1991 by Bill and Meredith Schroeder as a not-for-profit organization, MAQS is located in an expansive 27,000 square-foot facility, making it the largest quilt museum in the world. Its facility includes three exhibit galleries, four class-rooms, and a gift and book shop.

Through collecting quilts and other programs, MAQS focuses on celebrating and developing today's quiltmaking. It also provides a comprehensive program of exhibits, activities, events, and services to educate about the ever-developing art and tradition of quiltmaking. Whether presenting new or antique quilts, MAQS promotes understanding of, and respect for, all quilts – new and antique, tradi-tional and innovative, machine made and hand made, utility and art.

The MAQS exhibit galleries regularly feature a selection of the Museum's own collection of quilts made from the 1980s on, as well as exhibits of new and antique quilts and related archival materials. Workshops, conferences, and exhib-it-related publications provide additional educational opportunities. The Museum's shop carries a wide selection of fine crafts and hundreds of quilt and textile books.

Located in historic downtown Paducah, Kentucky, MAQS is open year-round 10 A.M. to 5 P.M. Monday through Saturday. From April 1 through October 31, it is also open on Sundays from 1 P.M. to 5 P.M.. The entire facility is wheelchair accessible.

MAQS programs can also be enjoyed on the website: www.quiltmuseum.org or through MAQS traveling exhibits like the annual New Quilts from an Old Favorites contest and exhibit. For more information, write MAQS, PO Box 1540, Paducah, KY 42002-1540; phone (270) 442-8856; or e-mail info@quiltmuseum.org.

95

Tumbling Blocks: New Quilts from an Old Favorite

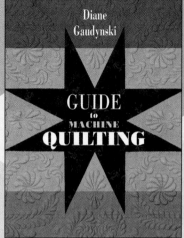

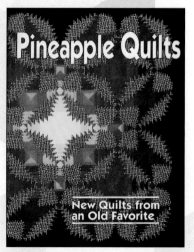